THE ENTREPRENEUR'S GUIDE
TO GROWING UP

THE ENTREPRENEUR'S GUIDE
TO GROWING UP

Taking your small company to the next level

Edna Sheedy

Self-Counsel Press
(*a division of*)
International Self-Counsel Press Ltd.

Printed in Canada

First edition: March, 1993

Canadian Cataloguing in Publication Data
Sheedy, Edna, 1939-
    The entrepreneur's guide to growing up
    (Self-counsel business series)
    Includes bibliographical references.

    ISBN 0-88908-549-8

    1. Small business—Management. 2. Entrepreneurship. I. Title. II.
Series.
    HD62.7.S53 1993   658.02'2   C93-091170-9

Cartoons by Dave Alavoine
Cover photography by Terry Guscott, ATN Visuals, Vancouver

BK
$8.95

Self-Counsel Press
(*a division of*)
International Self-Counsel Press Ltd.

1481 Charlotte Road	1704 N. State Street
North Vancouver, B.C.	Bellingham, WA
V7J 1H1	98225

Always Tim.

*And to Warwick Reid and Susan Baumgartner,
masters of commonsense management —
and good friends. You're the best.*

*And to all the terrific people I worked with at Elan.
Thanks for teaching me so much.*

*And to my son, Mitch, who used his head
for the good of his feet.*

CONTENTS

WORKSHEETS

SAMPLES

INTRODUCTION

Are you running Chaos Incorporated? Working harder, longer, and more energetically than you ever have, and still treading water? Maybe it's time to work smarter.

Chances are, you're an entrepreneur who didn't plan beyond getting your business started and making a decent profit. You never dreamed you'd be concerned about managing growth so soon. But here you are, the C.E.O. of a dynamic enterprise, faced with a challenge you didn't anticipate and don't feel quite ready for.

Your business is changing and growing under you, and all that shifting is making you queasy. You would prefer to be on surer ground.

It's time for some stocktaking.

First, let's agree on the definition of small business, and let's do it by the back door. That way you'll know if this book is worth the cover price.

Small business is *not* General Motors, IBM, AT&T, or any other organization that —

- has a whole department dedicated to personnel,
- maintains a library of A-to-Z procedure manuals,
- employs a score of professional managers,
- has a flawlessly detailed organization chart,
- has planning and budgeting departments, and
- runs a slick, effective computer systems group.

If you've already taken your business to this lofty plateau, you don't need this book. You probably should write one.

But if you're an owner-operator who —

- employs people or plans to,
- claims a few handwritten stabs at a policy manual stuffed in a "tomorrow file,"
- has managers trained from the ground up (and up isn't very high!),
- uses a floor layout for an organization chart,
- defines planning and budgeting as midnight oil, and
- has an overburdened computer run by a guy whose best work is promises and overtime...

read on.

This book makes some assumptions. The first is obvious. If the title of this book grabbed your attention, your business is growing — challenging your people, your internal systems, and, most of all, your management skills. Second, you have a strong desire to manage that growth wisely and well. And third, you're prepared to work hard for that objective.

There will be no squirming away from Truman's maxim about exactly where the buck stops. It's *your* goal, it's *your* responsibility, and it's no cakewalk. But it can be done. You may need to change long-held habits, review stale thinking, and stride boldly in some new directions. But you've come this far — what's another step or two?

No doubt you come to this book with preconceptions and a host of strong opinions; I've seldom met a businessperson without them. But I've never met a successful one who couldn't set those opinions aside for the time it takes to listen to new ones.

As a businessperson, you know that you need many diverse abilities to grow your business effectively. If you're honest, you'll admit that you don't have them all — yet. Each new step, each unexpected fork in the road brings questions, new issues, and sometimes disturbing challenges. To prosper, you must handle each of them while keeping a cool head and holding a steady course. It's your job, the job you created the day you opened for business.

What does it take? Two things in abundance.

First, common sense. No other attribute, no other skill, not one single other talent, learned or otherwise, casts a longer or more golden shadow on your enterprise than common sense. It is a fine lens that lets you foresee the results of action and reaction and make decisions accordingly. And there is nothing very common about it; it is in all too short a supply. It is also the root of the second essential to your continuing success: leadership.

Leadership is a complex amalgam of heart, strength, morality, rationality, and courage that attracts people of like mind to follow. It has nothing to do with giving orders, the power to hire and fire, or having financial clout. Leadership is a basic value that only you can bring to your business, and it is the intangible asset without which it will not endure.

This book aims to help you, the willing entrepreneur, grow as a manager and leader of your enterprise. To that end we will work, think, and smile, while we steal a page or two from the professional manager's handbook. Not too many, mind — just enough to make the ground stop trembling beneath your feet.

What's in this book worked for me. I hope it helps.

1
IN THE BEGINNING

Things are always at their best in their beginning.

Blaise Pascal

The small, privately held company most often finds its start in the mind and spirit of an entrepreneur: a person of drive, energy, and vision who creates a solid shape from a hazy idea.

"Damn the torpedoes — full speed ahead!" he or she yells, convinced that enthusiasm and fervor will win the day, and in the early days of business development, it often does. Guided by instinct and grit, the entrepreneur is as necessary to an embryonic enterprise as money in the bank — more so.

Starting a business takes boldness, brains, and bluff: boldness to seize opportunity, brains to analyze and keep score, and bluff to mask the weak spots. The successful entrepreneur has all of them in full measure. But things change, and often the skills used to start the business aren't enough to ensure it a full and profitable maturity. Running a dynamic organization makes unending and often unexpected demands on the unprepared business owner — and bluff only goes so far.

Smart entrepreneurs quickly recognize a simple truth: to effectively manage growth and fully enjoy its benefits, they must start thinking ahead. They need to identify where the business is now, where they want it to go in the future, and then decide how best to navigate the passage in between.

For the passage to be a smooth one, you need —

- a willingness to make personal change,

- openness to new ideas and concepts,
- clear, obtainable goals,
- a plan to meet those goals,
- an efficient organizational structure,
- the support of motivated employees,
- the ability to delegate, and
- easy access to pertinent, current information.

In this book, we'll touch on these needs, especially the first: your need to appraise and, if necessary, alter your role within the organization as it builds and changes. Everything begins with you. Your attitude is crucial and your decision making is the key to attaining profitable growth.

Start with a brief look back. Take a few moments to examine your roots and see where you've been. It will provide a standard to measure against, clear your thinking, and make a sound base for future decisions.

THOSE WERE THE DAYS

In the early days, you knew if you were making a profit by walking the production floor or touring the shipping area. You scanned the monthly sales, mentally subtracted your costs, and smiled. You knew how much cash was in the bank, what the payroll was going to be, and pretty much what to expect for the following month. There were few surprises and even fewer complexities. You saw and understood everything.

You didn't employ "staff," you worked with "people" — people who gave as much time and dedication to the fledgling enterprise as you did. You didn't have meetings back then, you had talks; meandering conversations that included hazy plans as well as the clear exchanges of information necessary in the running of the business. You shared, they shared, and you covered for each other. There were no roles, no parameters, and no hard and fast rules other than get the job done and do it right. Almost everyone in the place knew the status of everything that was going on. Knowledge was universal and shared willingly both from top to bottom and bottom to top. The best of everything and everyone went into building the company.

Consider for a moment exactly what the best was:

Was it attention to detail?
Was it a concern for quality?
Was it shared rewards?
Was it a prevailing team spirit?
Was it a genuine regard for the customer?
Was it enthusiasm?
Was it flexibility and innovative thinking?
Was it the fun, enjoyment, and camaraderie?

Take a trip down memory lane. Remember what was special about your business back then, and make note of it on Worksheet #1.

The idea is to keep the best of your beginnings and give it a professional polish. While we can never reclaim the past, we can learn from it by reviewing its lessons. Yesterday is a useful source for the insights we need to build a more secure future.

If you can't answer the why and how questions, leave them blank. Come back to them later after a little more thought.

Note: There will be other questions and worksheets throughout this book. Give them thought, effort, and honesty bordering on the brutal. If you're like most business owners, it's rare for you to take a few quiet minutes to review your performance or think about your future. You're doing it now; make the most of it. Think. Agree or disagree. Think again. Get a pen. Make notes. Cross things out. Doodle in the margins. Get involved.

WORKSHEET #1
MEMORY LANE

The characteristics that contributed the most to the success and excitement of my early days in business were:

_____

_____

_____

_____

_____

_____

Are they still at work in my business?   yes ____   no ____

Why?

_____

_____

_____

_____

Can I get them back?   yes ____   no ____

How?

_____

_____

_____

_____

STAYING SHARP

In those early days, your ability to quickly monitor the pulse of your business produced a comfort zone, facilitated decision making, and bolstered your confidence. When things weren't going well, you were flexible enough to make changes fast. And so were your people. What you had was an edge, a competitive edge.

Every day, large, established businesses lose customers to small, start-up companies with exactly this kind of edge: companies that are lean, fast, and resourceful. Quick-witted and brashly innovative, the owners of these small companies can and do clean up in the marketplace. But — and it's a big but — many of these hard-won customers go back where they came from when the entrepreneur fails, or arrogantly refuses, to develop the management expertise to maintain his or her advantage over the long haul. Put simply, they drop the ball.

Is there a message in this? You bet.

Unorganized growth blunts your edge.

How does it happen?

As a business grows, owners tend to spread themselves too thin by being, or trying to be, involved in everything. This scattering of energy and talent is unhealthy for the business, irritating to key people, and inhibiting to long-term success. Problems build with the creeping tenacity of root rot, and solutions can be long in coming. It seems like the company is operating in slow motion. The paradox is that you're still running to catch up!

Somewhere along the way it's imperative that you acquire the skill and tools to sharpen your edge and keep it that way. Rather than being *reactive,* a management style generally characterized by inconsistency, chaos, and wildly creative delaying tactics, become *proactive.* Develop a method that is innovative, anticipatory, and most important, consistent. Take control — and keep it.

If you're a cast-in-stone entrepreneur, you may have no interest in learning a bunch of tiresome management skills. The phrases information systems, teamwork, objectives, budgets, and long-term planning elicit only deep groans. That's fine, but be prepared, because with that attitude, the long haul will be perilous. But if, among all that instinct and grit, you can find some adaptability, then you'll find the road is high, wide, and straight.

THE HERE AND NOW

There comes a point in any small business when the old ways just don't cut it anymore. The methods and attitudes used to start a business are worn and tired. They did the job on the foundation, but you're on ground level now and moving

Business owners tend to spread themselves too thin.

9

upward. While you may be expert at pouring cement, erecting steel beams requires tools from a different trade.

At what point are you right now? Take a snapshot and see. To determine what you need to move forward, assess your present position and start thinking. Strive for objectivity and be tough on yourself and your organization. Worksheet #2 provides questions to spur the process. They are not intended as a quiz, but rather as a touchstone for the ideas that come out of this book — yours and mine.

GROWTH: THE FLIP SIDE

You want your business to fulfill its potential while laying a path for you to greater wealth and personal satisfaction. To do this your business must progress. It must grow. It may not be every businessperson's dream to run a billion-dollar multinational conglomerate, but most want at least modest increases in sales and profits as the years tick by. They accept change as a constant and both seek and savor the stimulation and challenges offered by forward movement.

Business growth as a goal is admirable. Can a free-market economy do anything but applaud the ambitions of the honest, growth-seeking entrepreneur? No. A growing business is not only good for its owner, it is a net contributor to the financial and personal well-being of its employees, suppliers, customers, and marketplace neighbors.

But how much of it are you ready for? Both your skills and confidence level are tested by a growing, changing business. With growth, your once-small company becomes multifaceted, new people are hired, new divisions formed, new offices are opened, and new ideas are tested. You are in uncharted territory. The adrenaline still pumps, the enthusiasm is still there, but it's dampened somewhat by stress and anxiety.

Growth in a small business does have a flip side. All the excitement and satisfaction that comes with success brings

WORKSHEET #2
THE SNAPSHOT

	Yes	No	Don't know
1. Is my company financially healthy?	___	___	___
2. Do I know what I need to keep it that way?	___	___	___
3. Is accounting timely and accurate?	___	___	___
4. Do I avoid stopgap problem-solving?	___	___	___
5. Are the company objectives clear?	___	___	___
6. Can I rally people to meet those objectives?	___	___	___
7. Do I make fact-based decisions?	___	___	___
8. Are my information needs being met?	___	___	___
9. Have I forged a clear chain of command?	___	___	___
10. Do I limit the number of people reporting to me?	___	___	___
11. Do I handle conflict quickly? Honestly?	___	___	___
12. Do I value and reward employee performance?	___	___	___
13. Do I plan for my business?	___	___	___
14. Is there a sense of teamwork in my company?	___	___	___
15. Can I identify my key people?	___	___	___
16. Are people trained to do their jobs?	___	___	___
17. Do people have the tools to do their jobs?	___	___	___
18. Do I provide a climate for growth?	___	___	___
19. Does the buck stop with me?	___	___	___
20. Am I committed to self-improvement?	___	___	___

new demands on you and your staff, and the pressure builds. Paperwork escalates. Time evaporates. People disappoint.

These are all healthy signs that your enterprise is alive and well, but you probably didn't plan for any one of them. And let's be frank, they're all problematic. Paperwork, time, and people need to be managed effectively if your small business is to prosper. Of the three, the people problem demands the most thought and sensitivity. Managing people to bring out their best for the company is the imperative to reaching success.

PEOPLE PROBLEMS — NO SUCH THING!

I have to say right here that I dislike the phrase people problem. I use it because it is the term often used by business owners when they need a scapegoat for their difficulties. Such owners would rather moan about inefficient, incompetent employees than face the possibility that they themselves are inept managers and poor leaders.

"Where's the work ethic?" they ask, adding woefully, "Nobody cares about quality anymore." They finish with the old classic, "If I want something done right, I have to do it myself." The business owner who makes this statement is probably right. If he or she truly believes no one else is up to the job, it's probably true. It is that business owner who has built a one-horse town, and he or she is the horse. There's not much chance the little town will amount to much. After all, one horse can only do so much.

So what's the message?

If you can't trust the people in your organization to do their jobs, to learn and grow with the company, growth will be stunted.

Another message? *Trust can be built.*

A growing business has a myriad of problems. They buzz about the owner's head like flies over fruit. Get rid of one; another takes its place. They seem constant, unavoidable, and maddeningly interchangeable. But problems are not people, and people are not problems if they are respected as employees, effectively motivated, and managed as the valuable resource they are.

Am I saying there's no such thing as a bad employee, only bad managers? No. I'm saying that with fair and consistent management methods, you can tip the odds in your favor.

As for that mountain of paperwork and evaporating time, they're first cousins; one comes with the other. You can get them under control — if and when you want to. Chances are, when it comes to dealing with the paperwork pile, your battery is low on charge. This is not exciting stuff, but it is important because it draws on your time. And nothing is more important than your time — other than how you choose to use it.

One of the first things to do is some analysis. Dig through that paper. Ask yourself what's important, what's not. Get your desk clean, lean, and ready for the challenges to come. You've got better things to do than paw through paper. And buy some books on time management. There are terrific ones out there with a thousand helpful hints.

(You might want to refer to *Practical Time Management*, another title in the Self-Counsel Series.)

WHAT'S YOUR PROBLEM?

In recent years, it's been unpopular to use the word *problem* when referring to business difficulties. In the effort to be always positive, the acceptable word has been *challenge*. But I don't buy it. Challenges excite, stimulate, provoke — make our blood race with anticipation. That repetitive error in shipping, perennially overdue financial statement, or everlastingly late employee are more inclined to make our blood boil. They're problems plain and simple, and it's best to deal with them quickly and directly or they'll grow like crab grass.

Webster's Dictionary tells us a problem is a "question raised for inquiry, consideration, or solution." In another definition, it says it's "a source of perplexity, distress, or vexation." I prefer the first definition; it implies you can bring influence to bear and encourages action. Let's customize it.

Every small business is as unique as the person who runs it. At any given time, the business owner has one or two problems weighing more heavily on the mind than others. And the problem with problems is that they grow right along with your company. Best to get rid of the perplexing, distressing, vexatious things. All it takes is a little mental vigor. So, without tongue in cheek, I'm asking, "What's your problem?"

Think about your most pressing current problem. Define it. Give it shape. It makes a better target that way. Who knows, maybe some of the ideas in this book will be the key to solving it.

My main business problem is:

_____

_____

_____

_____

_____

_____

_____

_____

How old is the problem? _____

Cause: _____

_____

_____

Action I've taken: _____

_____

_____

_____

_____

_____

TAKE A COMPANY X RAY

Now let's take another look at your snapshot, then we'll go deeper. Take a full X ray and examine the bones, the supporting structure of your company by completing Worksheet #3 now. The questions are meant to help you review what you know about your company and, more important, what you don't know. And remember, strive for honesty until it hurts.

No one but you can answer the questions, and your responses relate to you and your business only. You should be able to provide an answer for every question. If you can't, who will?

1. Is my company financially healthy?

   Define healthy: _____

   _____

   _____

2. Do I know what I need to keep it that way?

   Name three absolute necessities for continued growth:

   a. _____

   b. _____

   c. _____

3. Is accounting timely and accurate?

   The number of days after month end that you receive your financial reports is _____.
   You have not seen an error in the statements for the past _____ months. Are you satisfied with this? _____ If not, note the changes you would like:

   _____

   _____

   _____

4. Do I avoid stopgap problem solving?

   Give an example of a stopgap solution:

   _____

   _____

5. Are the company objectives clear?

   Name them: _____

   _____

   _____

   _____

6. Can I rally people to meet those objectives?

   Tell how: _____

   _____

   _____

7. Do I make fact-based decisions?

   Give an example and indicate source of facts:

   _____

   _____

   _____

8. Are my information needs being met?

   What do you need to know —

   Daily? _____

   _____

   Weekly? _____

   _____

   Monthly? _____

   _____

9. Have I forged a clear chain of command?

   Sketch your organization chart:

10. Do I limit the number of people reporting to me?

    List managers and supervisors in your organization:

    _____

    _____

    _____

    _____

    List number reporting directly to you: _____

    Percentage of total? _____

    Are you satisfied with this? _____

11. Do I handle conflict quickly? Honestly?

    Recent conflict: _____

    _____

    _____

Date you first heard about it: _____

Date you took action: _____

12. Do I value and reward employee performance?

The last date you praised an employee was _____

The person was: _____

You monitor performance fairly by using the following method: _____

_____

13. Do I plan for my business?

Describe it: _____

_____

_____

Date plan was last reviewed: _____

People involved: _____

_____

_____

14. Is there a sense of teamwork in my company?

Your team is formal _____ informal _____

Who participates in company decisions (names):

_____

_____

Date of last group session _____

15. Can I identify my key people?

    Name the first string: _____

    _____

    _____

    Name the second: _____

    _____

    _____

16. Are people trained to do their jobs?

    Dates of courses/seminars recently attended:

    _____

    _____

    Outline future training plans: _____

    _____

    _____

17. Do my people have the tools to do their jobs?

    Describe the tools required: _____

    _____

    _____

18. Do I provide a climate for growth?

    Describe that climate: _____

    _____

    _____

19. Does the buck stop with me?

    Tell why: _____

    _____

    _____

    _____

    Describe your primary responsibility: _____

    _____

    _____

    _____

20. Am I committed to self-improvement?

    List last three steps you have taken to expand your business knowledge:

    a. _____   date: _____

    b. _____   date: _____

    c. _____   date: _____

    List business publications subscribed to:

    _____

    _____

    _____

    List last two books read:

    _____

    _____

Your answers to the questions in Worksheet #3 are subjective, arising from conditions within *your* organization — no one else's. Your answers reveal more than just your strengths and weaknesses as a business owner. They show your priorities and hint at your philosophical base. Each of us, through time and exposure to the events around us, acquires a set of beliefs. These beliefs are assumed either consciously or unconsciously, and they are reflected daily in our attitudes, interests, and decisions.

Think about your belief system. Is it a positive force for your business? Can you build on it. Can people buy into it? Does it create trust? Is it upbeat and honorable? Describe it.

_____

_____

_____

_____

Now go back and review the X-ray questions you faltered over. If you feel a creeping weakness when those questions relate to your people and how you manage them, you have real work to do. Important work. Vital work.

Chapter Review

Growth *is* change. Your company won't grow profitably if you stay locked into an outmoded, expedient, or self-centered, management style. To move ahead and maintain that forward movement, you must keep the best of what you are: enthusiastic, creative, innovative, and fearless and buff it up with the learned skill of the professional manager.

- Appraise and, if necessary, be prepared to alter your role in the company as it grows and changes.
- Don't scatter your energy by trying to do everything; it dulls your competitive edge.
- Stop reacting; become proactive. Learn to think, plan, and do rather than do, think, and fix.
- Trust in your people; only together can you effectively grow the business.
- The ability to manage people is an imperative to your continued success.
- Management skills *can* be learned.

2
TOP DOG BLUES

He was a bold man that first eat an oyster.

Jonathan Swift

We've all heard the expression, "It's lonely at the top." Well, it is. The man or woman who is head of a busy growing enterprise is very much alone. A good partner helps, good employees help, but the ultimate responsibility for the business is on the shoulders of its owner, and the load gets heavy.

*The ultimate responsibility for the business is
on the shoulders of its owner.*

As a small business owner, chances are you have had no formal business training other than what you've gleaned by reading and occasional seminars. You may only have a high school education — or less. If so, you are among the majority. Statistics from the United States Small Business Administration show that grade eleven is the average educational level for people starting a business. And many people with university educations are in businesses unrelated to their degree.

What does this mean? Does it mean most business owners have no idea what they are doing? That they got where they are today solely on luck and pluck? Does it mean anyone can do it? That starting and running a small business is child's play?

No. It means you, as a successful entrepreneur, have grown beyond the spirit of enterprise that initially propelled you into business, reached deep into your bag of skills and used every last one of them with flair and proficiency. And, although each step you took was new, each judgment untried, and each decision without a comforting history, you built a viable business. You've proven yourself; you've made it.

This should give you all the confidence you need to move forward, but often it does not. With no one to give you an A+ and pass you to the next grade, and no one to acknowledge your skills, accomplishments, or professional integrity, you may be convinced you owe your success to luck and happenstance. Instead of feeling bolstered by your success, perhaps you are overwhelmed and increasingly edgy. After all, if you truly feel success is bestowed on you by some capricious spirit, it can be taken back just as easily. Right?

Wrong! Let's get it straight. You've *earned* your success, and you *deserve* its rewards — and you are entitled to more. Luck had nothing to do with it.

Many small business owners wage silent, ongoing battles against personal insecurity. Through the years, they've managed to build only a thin crust of self-confidence and it is easily cracked.

Take the case of John, who, on the surface, is a brilliant success. From a difficult start in his garage three years ago, he has built a successful business manufacturing and installing custom mufflers. Now he operates in three locations. But even as the patents pend and the orders grow, he feels less and less sure of his ability to cope with the new dynamics at work in his business. He wonders how long his "luck" will last. He becomes overanxious when faced with bigger and more complex decisions.

John can neither forget nor reconcile himself to his lack of a formal education. Outwardly, he maintains it doesn't matter and may even say he's proud of what he's accomplished without it; inwardly, it chews at him, making him feel dangerously vulnerable. He is self-reliant, but not self-confident.

To move ahead, you must forge stronger armor. You need self-confidence and a sustaining belief in yourself and your abilities. Employees rely on it, suppliers trust it, and customers demand it. You need to believe you can do it — that the power is yours to seize and wield. There is nothing to hold you back if you believe in yourself and have a powerful commitment to shape your future.

Lack of education will not hold you back. Lack of management training will not hold you back. Past mistakes will not hold you back — unless you let them.

You've come this far because you've worked hard and paid your dues. I repeat — you've earned your success, and you deserve its rewards. You have reason to face your business future with optimism and in anticipation of even greater success.

As for luck, consider this: Stephen Leacock, the noted Canadian humorist, once said, "I'm a great believer in luck and I find the harder I work the more I have of it."

GROWING CONFIDENCE

Self-confidence comes from examining and internalizing our own accomplishments. Think of it as taking on fuel. By reflecting on and ingesting our successes, we become stronger and gain trust in ourselves and our abilities. It puts our insecurities as owner-managers into perspective and gives us the needed boost to step boldly on the next rung of the ladder.

Please, don't misunderstand me, I am not suggesting the development of an oversized ego that exacts homage and accolades every step along the way. That would not only be counterproductive, it would be self-destructive. True self-confidence is a healthy outgrowth of a much wiser, more constructive ego. Nurtured properly, it builds inner power and provides crucial support as you step toward a more demanding future.

It's not often you're asked to blow your own horn. But this is one of those times. On Worksheet #4, make a list of your accomplishments, highlight your successes, and tally your wins. No doubt you will be surprised at the list of your accomplishments. This is a list for you alone. It has one purpose: to make you feel good about the distance you've traveled and to prepare you for the miles to come. If you can't bring yourself to write them down, list them in your mind and savor each and every one. Call it your win list and add to it often.

I hope you fill the page, but if you don't, give yourself a pat on the back anyway. You are still in business, and given that the failure rate for small business is close to 90% in the first year of operation, you're definitely doing something right.

I have immense respect for the doers of this world, those enterprising, action-oriented people who step front and center to lead the pack while everyone around them wails and criticizes.

"It's not right," they cry.

WORKSHEET #4
WIN LIST

_____

_____

_____

_____

_____

_____

_____

_____

_____

_____

_____

_____

_____

_____

_____

_____

_____

_____

_____

_____

"*I* would have done it this way," they intone.

"I could have done it better," they sniff.

Yes, well, *they* haven't done it at all. You have. The way I see it, we need a lot more of you and a lot less of them.

NEVER ENOUGH KNOWLEDGE

Business owners often shortchange themselves when it comes to increasing their general knowledge or growing leadership skills. After a while, this inattention puts them out of step with changing times and further erodes their self-confidence. Either they place no value on learning, or they tell themselves they don't have the time for it. Worse yet, many of them believe they already know it all — or at least everything they need to know to run their operation. Stale thinking. Risky thinking.

Knowledge is not merely information on the how and what of things. It is a broader understanding comprised of learning, wisdom, experience, awareness, intelligence, discernment, insight, appreciation, and enlightenment. Knowledge is the air your business breathes, and you need to ensure it circulates freely throughout your organization. While you're at it, take some deep breaths yourself.

Understand that the knowledge you need is not found within the walls of your office. It is too vast, too universal in scope, to be so confined. Remember too, it is available to your competitors in equal measure. Who takes the most and uses it wisely, wins.

The nature of small business requires that its owner be a well-informed generalist. There is the need to recognize trends and to differentiate between passing fads and the far-reaching changes that will affect your enterprise. And there is the need to ground your decisions in an ethical base that will strengthen it over the long term.

Your business is silk in the web, part of a delicate, interwoven construction affected by politics, changing mores, environmental concerns, consumer moods, government legislation, demographics, social customs, buying habits, immigration, technology, the aging population... The list is endless, and not all of it is quantifiable or easily packaged into meaningful statistics. But being aware of such influences may save you from some serious blunders along the way.

Consider A.J., the owner and operator of a retirement waterfront mobile home park. For over ten years, she had owned fifty acres of land along the water, eight of it being used for the mobile park. A couple of years ago, an environmental group had pressured the local government to buy the excess land as a wildlife refuge. It was a decent enough offer but A.J. had no desire to sell. As the area grew, it made sense for her to develop further acreage into parking for the many recreational vehicles visiting the area every tourist season.

She saw a need and set about to fill it. What she didn't foresee was the environmental storm that followed her decision. The community, along with every environmental group within a 500-mile radius, was incensed at the idea of anything that would affect the natural state of A.J.'s waterfront acreage. Plans were stalled and construction delayed as two levels of government were dragged into the fight. In the end, a compromise was reached. A.J. got a cut-down version of her mobile home park and the government bought another park. It was a costly lesson for A.J. and one that might have been avoided had she been more aware of the pitfalls.

Commitment to self-improvement, learning, and the scholarship of enterprise is basic to good leadership. As a leader you must stay informed and innovative. You need ideas, creativity, and inspiration as much in the day-to-day operation of your business as you did when you began it. You need knowledge, and it doesn't come neatly sandwiched between telephone calls and meetings. While you don't have to climb a mountain and meditate (although if you do have the time, it's not such a bad idea), you do need breathing room and outside stimuli to revitalize the process of innovation and creative thought.

STAY IN TOUCH WITH THE WORLD

If it has been a while since you attended a seminar, you might want to start there. Look for a good one and reach. Don't just sign up for a half-day course on statistical analysis or how to get the most out of your financial statement. While these are good practical endeavors, they aren't enough to jolt the imagination and revitalize your vision.

Reach! Learn about any of these:

- Creativity

- Ethics

- Business strategy

- Personal development

Commitment to self-improvement, learning, and
the scholarship of enterprise is basic to good leadership.

31

- Environmental issues
- Communication
- Technology
- Politics
- Philosophy
- Time management
- Innovative management techniques
- Decision-making
- Problem-solving techniques
- Meditation
- Leadership
- History

Widen your focus to include the study of other businesses. Stay aware of innovations in other industries. Become active in your local board of trade, chamber of commerce, and any other business group where you will encounter diverse people and opinions.

Don't have time? Make some. You won't regret it.

Companies in industries other than yours may be initiating new, exciting approaches to business that will work equally as well for you. So step outside your normal boundaries and let your mind explore. As leader of the organization, a big part of your job is to look for the concepts, information, and new ideas that will keep your business in the front line. It is high-priority work.

Your company was founded on the strength of an idea, and it will be ideas that sustain it. New, exciting ideas invigorate and enliven the whole organization. Give yourself the time and opportunity to find them.

Aside from the fact that good ideas translate into happy employees, bottom-line dollars, and an increase in your confidence, there's an added bonus: motivation — yours.

Education is not a destination; it is an ongoing journey. Learning, going down new roads, and meeting and exchanging ideas with fellow travelers renews you. By reawakening your spirit of adventure and broadening your perspectives, it encourages you to set higher goals and work to them.

Admit it. The day-to-day routine of business gets dull, and it's tempting to drift for a while. When things are good, there's little incentive to scan new horizons or make changes. Everything's fine. Profits are up, and things are comfortable. Ho-hum.

Profits are not synonymous with motivation. Our spirits crave more substantial incentive. If your business has slipped into neutral, and you don't do something about it, your next big challenge will likely be staying awake long enough to count the mushroom crop. So don't settle down, don't settle in, and don't settle for comfort. Your business is under silent siege. Buffeted from within and without, it is set upon by a killjoy economy, unsettled markets, and shifting values. To exist and grow in such unpredictable conditions, it — and you — must be at the ready. The only weapon you have or will ever have is knowledge.

Get some, anywhere you can. And keep on getting it as long as you run your business.

On Worksheet #5, make a list of topics of interest and put a date beside each item. Tell yourself that by this date you will have found a source of instruction on the topic.

Then use Worksheet #6 to start a reading list. Go to the library and start touring the bookstores again. The business section is alive with bright covers and even brighter ideas. Jot some of the more interesting titles down and buy at least one or two. If they're the right ones, you'll want to refer to them again and again. Once you've read the book, you may want to make note of any particularly noteworthy ideas or concepts. A discussion of these ideas with your people can often bring surprisingly productive results.

Chapter Review

If this chapter leaves you with but one thought, let it be that as the owner of a business you can never stop learning and never stop opening your mind to new experiences and people. Perhaps John F. Kennedy put it best when he said, "Leadership and learning are indispensable to each other." They are the perfect partners to forge a strong future.

- You have earned your success; you deserve its rewards.

- A healthy degree of self-confidence is necessary to move your company forward.

- You can grow your confidence by growing your knowledge.

- Without fresh ideas and stimuli, you and your business risk stagnation.

WORKSHEET #5
THE KNOWLEDGE I WANT

Topic	Date
_____	_____
_____	_____
_____	_____
_____	_____
_____	_____
_____	_____
_____	_____
_____	_____
_____	_____
_____	_____
_____	_____
_____	_____
_____	_____
_____	_____
_____	_____
_____	_____
_____	_____

WORKSHEET #6
MY READING PLAN

Title	Comment
_____	_____
_____	_____
_____	_____
_____	_____
_____	_____
_____	_____
_____	_____
_____	_____
_____	_____
_____	_____
_____	_____
_____	_____
_____	_____
_____	_____
_____	_____
_____	_____
_____	_____
_____	_____

3
TAKING AIM

It takes little talent to see clearly what lies under one's nose, a good deal of it to know in which direction to point that organ.

W.H. Auden

I know successful people who swear they've never set a goal in their business lives — and they've got along just fine, thank you. They take pride in this accomplishment and defend their position by saying goals make you inflexible. They maintain that by specifying the objective, you can bypass opportunity — even miss the main chance. They would have you believe they drift along picking opportunities at will from the playful hand of fate. Whatever skill they have, they modestly add, is solely an ability to respond to what's offered and make the most of it.

They are wrong.

They do set goals, every day, every month and every year. If you were to ask that businessperson what the expected sales for the month are, or where the business will be in five years, there's a good chance he or she will tell you in depth. No matter what words couch it, how hesitantly he or she puts it forth, or how foggy it may appear, it is a goal. By defining goals, you clear away the fog and a great deal of uncertainty.

IDENTIFY YOUR TARGET

Setting goals for your company does not mean locking yourself to a rigid schedule or donning blinkers that preclude seeing new opportunities. It simply means thinking deeply about what you want for, and from, your organization, then focusing your time and energy on achieving it.

Corporate goals should —

- *make sense.* It doesn't make sense to plan an assault on Mount Everest if you've never climbed before. It doesn't make sense to be planning an acquisition program the day after the bank calls in your loans. It doesn't make sense to aim to increase your business by price cutting if you're already selling at below cost. When you set goals, use your head and a goodly portion of logic.

- *be worth the effort.* Chances are that a plan to maintain sales will not set many hearts to pounding. Goals should make you want to work toward them and offer real value to you, your people, and the company. Certainly, financial reward will form a large part of this value, but it need not be all. Goals can be enhanced by adding a new dimension. Consider a social or charitable aspect as a worthwhile by-product. It will strengthen motivation.

- *be clearly defined.* Write them down, black on white. Be concise, definite, and specific. Don't waffle. Give your goals color and substance. You'll need to review them from time to time; it helps when they're shaped in something more substantial than wet sand and smoke.

- *have the support of your key people.* This is the number-one imperative. Your goals must be clear enough, logical enough, and have value enough to encourage and maintain support. Think shared benefits, not self-gratification.

- *require energetic action.* Goals should require the doing of something — something beyond what you do now. They should demand your best and require you to stretch. Goals should take you up and inspire you, so that when, after those first faltering steps, you reach them, you can't wait to set them higher still.

- *be prioritized.* All goals are not created equal. Recognize what should come first and act accordingly. See which goal is dependent on the successful attainment of another. Think them through.

- *be attainable.* Do not set goals so high you need wings to scratch bottom. It's pointless and discouraging to have a goal that's always out of reach. It's nice if you can reach your goals in this lifetime.

- *be measurable.* Of course, you'll know when you finally attain your goal, but it's a good idea to build in a few checkpoints along the way. Make a note of how close you plan to be to your objective at one month, six months, a year, and so on, and review your progress.

FIRST STEPS

Goal setting is neither complicated nor mysterious, it is simply a learned discipline rooted in common sense. For the entrepreneur who would be a more professional and effective manager, it is the first solid step toward that objective.

In a large organization, establishing goals is often a cool and dispassionate activity dominated by hidebound policy and the economic objectives of the corporation. The process has form but no fire.

In the small company, financial goals are not always preeminent. In fact, the astute small business owner prefers the monetary objective to be a by-product of goals centering on improved service, product quality, productivity gains, or employee-incentive programs. They rightly believe that by working toward a healthier tree they are assured of bountiful fruits. Such corporate goals are easily shared and find ready support among dedicated employees who have a real interest in the success of the company.

Support is critical to attaining corporate goals. Face it, Mr. Do-all in production isn't going to care if all you want is to add a million dollars to your bank account. Why should he? What's in it for him? But if your goal is to improve productivity in his department by 20% — and you're proposing he share in the gains from that improvement — you'll no doubt get his full cooperation. Enlisting the necessary support early in the goal-setting process goes a long way to actualization.

Fear of failure, of not measuring up, deters many businesspeople from clearly defining goals. At least it stops them from writing goals down. There is definitely something intimidating about writing down goals that first time. For one thing it takes away your ability to fudge, sidestep, and deny if events don't unfold as planned. And while it does take courage to raise expectations and set yourself up to be judged by the world's most exacting critic — you — it's worth the risk.

Those few lines scratched on paper are a first step toward a more professional approach to managing your company, and they act as a rallying point for employees by motivating and focusing them on a common objective. Shared goals are the foundation of teamwork, and teamwork is the engine of growth.

SETTING YOUR GOALS

Worksheet #7 is a "wish inventory." It provides a starting point for the goal-setting process. Start by pulling your hopes, dreams, and incomplete plans from the misty corners of your mind and giving them a rough shape — and relax. It will take time to turn your wish inventory into a set of concrete goals, and you will probably discard many of your first entries when common sense and logic kick in. What you're doing now is a long way from formulating the specific goals you will be

WORKSHEET #7
WISH INVENTORY

Next week, I'd like to: _____

_____

_____

_____

In about six months or so, I'd like to: _____

_____

_____

_____

By this time next year, it would be ideal if: _____

_____

_____

_____

I've had this idea ... _____

_____

_____

_____

The thing I want most of all is _____

_____

_____

_____

discussing with your people later on. For now, concentrate on making your dreamscape a navigable landscape, and keep your mind open to new ideas as they come to you. Fill in the blanks, and don't worry about it if what you write doesn't make much sense.

After you've filled it in, review your wish inventory. Think deeply. Discard the unattainable. Discard the nonsensical. Firm it up.

Consider your "wishes" within the practical framework of your organization: the costs, the benefits, the people, information, and systems required to attain them.

Then, in Worksheet #8, write down three solid, sensible, valuable goals for your organization in order of priority. Define them clearly by writing short, complete sentences with positive action verbs. Indicate a rough timeline for their achievement. But remember, these are company goals; discussion with your people is necessary before a firm schedule can be set.

After you've finished that task, move to Worksheet #9 to review each of the goals.

PEOPLE POWER

If you honestly answered yes to the questions in Worksheet #9, begin now to consider the people in your organization. Let your thoughts filter down through your first level of management, second level, etc. Who will your goals affect? Who will benefit?

Whose support is critical to goal attainment?

Jot down names:

_____

_____

_____

_____

WORKSHEET #8
COMPANY GOALS

Goal #1: _____

_____

_____

_____

_____

Timeline: _____

_____

Goal #2: _____

_____

_____

_____

_____

Timeline: _____

_____

Goal #3: _____

_____

_____

_____

_____

Timeline: _____

_____

WORKSHEET #9
GOAL REVIEW

Review the goals again, then answer the following questions for each of them.

	Goals		
	1	2	3
1. Does it tend toward solving an immediate problem *as well* as producing a positive long-term result?	___	___	___
2. Does it contribute to the greater good of the company? (Improve service, quality, productivity?)	___	___	___
3. Does it have a worthwhile by-product? (societal, charitable?)	___	___	___
4. Do you desire it strongly?	___	___	___
5. Will it stir you to act?	___	___	___
6. Can you commit to it for the long haul?	___	___	___
7. Can you get support for it?	___	___	___
8. Is it clearly defined (understandable)?	___	___	___
9. Is it ethical?	___	___	___
10. Is there a shareable reward when it is reached?	___	___	___

Look at your goals again. Are they clear enough to kick off a meeting with the people you have identified? If not, refine them further, then get together with your people.

At that meeting discuss your thoughts and goals openly, be straightforward about what you want for the company and the changes required. Ask for their input and ideas; most important, ask for their support. Outline clearly all benefits accruing to them when the goals are met. If this activity is a new experience for your people, leave a lot of time for questions. If there is doubt or cynicism about your intentions, address it.

Don't make the same mistake that one growing software firm did. Immediately after attending a two-day seminar called "Target — Your Future," the two senior partners in the company closeted themselves in an office and for the first time in the company's short history, established written goals and strategies for the coming year. They were enthusiastic and thorough.

They worked out a schedule, a budget, and documented their plan in impressive detail. When it was completed to their satisfaction, a copy of the document was given to each of their four managers. The last sentence said something about "requiring the managers' full cooperation." Dry as oatmeal.

The document was met with full-scale inertia and a healthy measure of resentment. It became a subject for criticism and some rather caustic office humor. In short, the managers hated it.

Why? Because they were excluded. They were left out of a process that affected their divisions, their plans, and their people. They were asked to perform but not participate, so they refused to buy into the program.

It isn't enough for you to believe your corporate goals are right and worthwhile; your people must share that belief. Include them wherever and whenever you can. If the goals stand up to their hard scrutiny, you've hit the first note. If, by the end of the process, your goal has become theirs, you're as good as there.

If they don't buy the whole program, go back a step or two. Listen to their arguments, reconsider, and discuss.

Before you take one step on the path to your goals be sure you have the people power to get you there.

Chapter Review

Create a program that will benefit everyone. Work with your people, and once they have chosen to get behind your company goals, get behind them. Give them the support they need to get the job done. Together you are an unstoppable force.

- Setting clear, obtainable goals strengthens the organization by focusing on the future.

- Goal setting is a learned discipline.

- The best goals are shared goals.

- The successful goal-setting program is powered by people.

4
A MATTER OF ARRANGEMENT

Before I built a wall I'd ask to know
What I was walling in or walling out.

Robert Frost

Many small companies go through the early years with neither formal structure nor clearly outlined chain of command. Everybody plays all the bases, and in most cases, it doesn't matter who's on first or who's on second, the job gets done. By and large, it works, but not forever.

The loose, undisciplined game plan starts to break down as more people are hired, specialized skills are added, more business is transacted, and more ambitious goals are set. Suddenly, people are bumping into each other at every turn. No one is quite sure of what their job is or where it stands in the company hierarchy. Nerves fray, anxieties surface, and employees reroute their mental energy away from getting the job done to figuring out a personal survival strategy. Amidst this confusion, quality suffers and errors are made. You begin to hear expressions like:

"John said he would take care of it?"

"Was I supposed to do that?"

"Sorry."

"I don't know."

"It's not my job."

"No one told me."

After hearing enough of the above, you soon decide a revitalized organization is not only necessary, but crucial to the well-being of your company.

The act of drawing the corporate organizational chart has been gruesomely described as "putting people in boxes." Put that way, it does sound rather terminal. As a determined, successful entrepreneur, no doubt the expression makes you shudder. Wasn't this exactly what you wanted to avoid by starting your own company? You had no plan to box either yourself or your employees into an oppressive structure stifling to both initiative and the free exchange of ideas. What you wanted was an openness that encourages sharing and communication, not walls to shut them out.

Excellent. But think for a moment about those expressions quoted above. Look at them from a different angle — that of your people. Isn't it possible your frustration in listening to this barrage of rationalizations and justifications is matched, and maybe surpassed, by the person forced to offer them as excuses for mistakes and poor performance? I believe it is. Organizing and describing the work to be done goes a long way toward eliminating such frustration, yours and theirs.

JOB DESCRIPTIONS

Intelligent people have a healthy degree of self-interest — they strongly desire to do well. Tapping into this desire is the first rule of good management. It follows then that if people do not want to fail, one of your million responsibilities as C.E.O. is to help them avoid it. When you are successful, you both win. Unclear, confusing working relationships do not contribute to this goal. Each of us needs to know our place in the corporate universe. Have you told your people where their places are?

Ask yourself:

- Do people know what their jobs are?

- Are the job descriptions in writing?

- Have the job descriptions been reviewed lately?

- Do people know who they report to?

- Do people know who reports to them?

- When hiring, can I fully describe the available position?

Business owners can be in for a shock when they sit down with an employee and discuss the day-to-day tasks of his or her job. Given time, growth, unexpected demands, and lack of consistent management, jobs tend to reconstruct themselves, and often bear no resemblance to the original mandate. You may find Mary in production doing typing for the sales department, or Jim in sales pitching in during busy times in the shipping department. Lines get smudged as the slack in a small company is picked up by willing, industrious employees.

This is both good and bad. Obviously the work needs to be done, but equally obvious is the need to plan and organize the work to ensure accountability and recognition. As more and more people are hired, more lines are crossed, and more detailed specifications of a job are required. At this point, the job description becomes a useful, hardworking management tool. It keeps you abreast of the work currently being performed in your company, while making a clear statement to the employee of what is expected of him or her in the job. It is an invaluable aid during performance reviews and makes the hiring task smoother and less prone to misunderstanding and error.

At the hiring stage, it is important not to mislead or confuse a potential applicant. The job interview is when expectations meet requirements; they seldom mesh. As well, there is often a tendency for applicants to hear only what they want to hear about the available position. I remember one owner of a small business who, after an exhaustive and expensive search for a salesperson to open a new territory, finally choose a man he thought was perfect for the job. Within a month there was a problem. It seems the owner saw the job as comprised mainly of prospecting and cold calls, while the new salesperson thought he was being hired to sit at a desk and develop a marketing plan. It took a lot of talking and even more compromise to work it out.

By trusting only your verbal skills to describe the position you are trying to fill, you leave a great deal to chance. It is to the benefit of the applicant and the employer to work with written guidelines when discussing any available position.

A job description can be as detailed or as general as you wish, but it must be an objective and very clear portrait of the position. Don't leave room for misunderstanding.

When first developing job descriptions, try not to have your attempt unduly colored by the person currently holding the job. For example, if you find that Sally in payroll is spending a lot of her time working on proposals for the sales department, it's unlikely you will want that task written into her accounting-based job description. Let common sense and logic prevail.

WHAT'S IN A TITLE?

Job titles are important. Choosing and assigning them takes care and thought. In the early days, for many small companies, choosing job titles is a willy-nilly affair at best. It isn't until the company expands that the consequences of this *ad hoc* approach comes back to haunt the business owner. Why, he or she wonders, was the first salesperson called *sales manager* or the first bookkeeper, *accounting manager*? They can barely manage themselves, let alone others. Some business people give titles in lieu of higher pay, or they believe bigger titles make the company sound larger than it is. Whatever the reason, it is short-term thinking. As the company grows, for the sake of truth and clarity, job title inconsistencies must be corrected.

Instituting any change within your company calls for empathy and tact, but never more so than when that change directly affects an individual's pride. An employee's place in the organization is important to the individual. If he or she perceives that the position is being downgraded, bitterness will often follow, and bitterness is slow poison for the small company.

When job title adjustments are part of a general reorganization, bitterness is dissipated somewhat by the fact that no one person is being singled out; there is solace in being part of a larger, less personally directed change. Still it is a sensitive task, and one you should fully prepare for should the need arise. Think about the following case.

Let's assume that you have a small sales department, say two people. The first employee in was Cody James, so when you hired the second person, Cody became sales manager. It seemed logical at the time, but in fact, the only management act Cody performs is to review the second person's expense report, and that's usually late getting to accounting. Cody doesn't like paperwork. His job is still mainly making calls and servicing his customers. He hasn't learned much from any of the training seminars you've sent him on.

Your company is growing, and within the next 12 months, you plan to hire 3 more salespeople. The problem? Cody James is one crackerjack sales representative, but no way does he have the management skills necessary to handle an expanded sales force. What are your options?

Leave Cody as sales manager and wait for him to fail. (Translation: I haven't got the courage to face the situation.)

Leave Cody as sales manager, but tell him you're going to help him out by getting more involved. (Translation: I'm going to do his job for him.)

Tell Cody your plans, explain that you are redefining the job description and upgrading the requirements for the sales manager's position, and *level with him* by doing the following:

(a) Assure him of his value to the company.

(b) Explain the reasons behind your decision, why you are doing this and why you are doing it now.

(c) If you believe there is a chance for him to grow his management skills working with a seasoned professional, tell him that. Don't slam the door on his future.

(d) Tell him what his new title will be (perhaps Senior Sales Representative?) and be clear about what that title entails.

(e) If he expresses concerns about his future with your company, respond forthrightly and with candor.

(f) Reassure him that this change is necessary because of company needs, ("the larger picture") not simply because he's doing a poor job.

Will the above steps guarantee Cody James will remain a happy, productive member of your staff? No. But, if he's intelligent and fair, it will ensure that he won't cut and run. He'll give you, and the coming changes, a chance. The rest will depend on that new sales manager you hire. (We'll talk about that at the end of this chapter.)

If you need to review your organization and job descriptions, do it as soon as possible. To avoid difficult situations like the above, always keep the following in mind: *A title should clearly reflect the job it is assigned to.* This gives it genuine value in the employee's eyes, and gives your customers and suppliers an understanding of that employee's authority within the organization. When a title means and says something, it is doing the work it should. Regard each job title in your company as a communication tool and you'll be on the right track.

Following are two samples to help you develop job descriptions in your company. Sample #1 represents the standard format for a job description. It asks for position title, the title of the position the job reports to, a summary statement, and a list of duties to be performed. The "date reviewed" line at the top of the page is used to indicate the last time the work associated with the job description was reviewed — not the employee holding down the job. Job descriptions should be reviewed and updated annually.

Sample #2 is a general job description for a generic manager. Note that I have underlined the directive phrases as a guide. These phrases are the basis of most job descriptions.

REVIEW, REASSESS, REEXAMINE

Before thinking of the broader, strategic decisions necessary to chart your organization, make sure you have up-to-date knowledge.

Reassess the activities that go on in the company. Review job titles. If no job descriptions are in place, work with your people to develop them. Explain what you want to do, why you want to do it, then start by having the existing job holder make a list of his or her duties. No one knows a job better than its incumbent, and no one is more important to the process of developing effective job descriptions.

Whether or not you choose to update your existing company structure or do a complete reorganization to allow for more expansion, refreshing your memory and heightening your senses to your current operation is always rewarding.

THE ORGANIZATION CHART

At some point, your growing company needs a comfortable, workable structure — a form to foster progress, encourage responsibility, and identify the players. In the beginning it may be only a rough sketch dealing with a half-dozen people, but that sketch should clearly show the skeleton of your

SAMPLE #1
JOB DESCRIPTION FORM

Date reviewed: _____

Title of position: _____

Reports to: _____

General description of job: _____

_____

_____

_____

_____

Specific duties:

1. _____

2. _____

3. _____

4. _____

5. _____

6. _____

7. _____

8. _____

9. _____

10. _____

Date reviewed: August 25, 19—

Title of position: Manager

Reports to: General Manager

General description of job:

To plan, organize, direct, and control the activities of the service department through staff at or above supervisory level. The manager is responsible for all operations within his or her department.

Specific duties:

1. To implement and recommend changes in procedure to achieve departmental goals.

2. To prepare and submit departmental budgets for approval.

3. To select and approve staff and direct training.

4. To coordinate activities with other departments.

5. To prepare all necessary reports.

6. To assist staff with problems, administrative or technical.

7. To negotiate with technical specialists and consultants for outside service selection.

company and allow for future growth. Such a sketch will go a long way toward bringing order and efficiency back to the fore, and you don't even have to draw boxes.

Sample #3 shows a couple of organization charts. Take a look. Which one most closely resembles yours?

The structure you design for your company will generally follow the basic form in the upper chart of Sample #3. It is straightforward, the titles and roles make sense, and there are no overlapping responsibilities. We can easily see who is responsible for what. When the company expands further, it will be a simple task to build on it. As for the lower chart in the sample, it's more a maze than a chart. Put simply, it's a mess; nonsensical reporting lines, crossover responsibilities, and no clear hierarchy. If your company chart looks like this, spill coffee on it, put it out of its misery, and start fresh.

Certainly you can adjust your organizational chart to meet your specific needs and the continuing demands of growth. Keep a simple framework that will allow you to add and subtract as necessary. While you can't know the precise organization that will serve all your future needs, work to keep your options open. Try to create a structure that works for the company and its people. Don't hesitate to customize it to suit your company, no matter how eccentric or unconventional.

Underlying the workable company organization are certain principles and a lot of good sense.

(a) No one has two bosses. One is more than most of us can handle. Having a double reporting line is a breeding ground for excuses and buck passing. If someone must wear two hats, prioritize responsibilities, organize so the second hat is worn in a special project scenario, and itemize the terms of the project. When and if the second hat needs to sit on a full-time head, hire one.

56

SAMPLE #3
CHARTING YOUR ORGANIZATIONAL STRUCTURE

It should look like this:

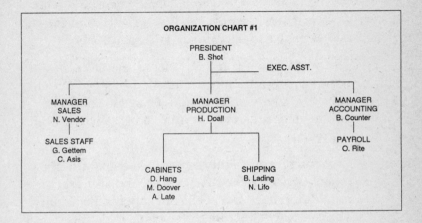

Not like this:

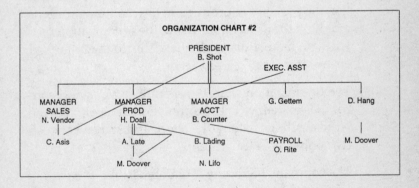

(b) Authority — over whom, what, where, and when — is defined and spelled out. Authority over people, places, or things is always an earned privilege and all authority should have limits and guidelines.

(c) Accountability — to whom, what, where, and when — is clear and unequivocal. An efficient organization allows people to measure up fairly and visibly.

(d) The organization is fully disclosed and all roles and positions are mutually understood by everyone involved. There must be no hidden agenda, no "pets," and no under-the-table "plum" projects handed out without discussion.

(e) The structure efficiently serves the people within the organization, not the other way around. It clears communication lines and spells out support availability. The company structure frees people to do their jobs; it does not constrain them.

(f) The structure is not so rigid that it inhibits innovation or cross-department input. There is room to breathe. If in the past, Jim in production has made suggestions that help the sales department, the organization provides a channel that will allow this to continue and ensure Jim is recognized accordingly.

(g) The organization chart covers all key tasks and contributes to their efficient completion. It recognizes the basic algebraic axiom: the shortest distance between two points is a straight line.

(h) The company hierarchy is plainly visible. The path to achievement is signposted, showing each person what is attainable given effective performance in his or her current job.

(i) The structure has no invisible walls barring competence and talent on the basis of race, creed, or sex.

The organizational structure of the small company is dynamic. While it must be strong, it should be flexible enough to allow today's free-thinking employee room to exercise his or her judgment as it pertains to daily work, while at the same time sustaining individual involvement in the company as a whole.

HIRING MANAGEMENT FROM OUTSIDE

Reviewing your company's structure and looking at the work being done often points out inadequacies and missing links — yours and your existing staff's. There may be a weakness in the customer support area:

- Quality is slipping.
- Complaints are not being handled.

The problem may be in marketing:

- There's a falloff in new business.
- There's no effective follow-up.
- Plans and ideas are on hold because you can't get to them.
- New markets are left to competitors.

Or it may lie in finance:

- Financial information is always late.
- Budgets and projections don't get done.
- Administrative errors are constant.
- Invoices go out late.

You decide you need newer, better management. If you're going to keep the ground you've gained and add more, you need experienced, top-notch help.

Fair play and logic tell you that you must first look in-house for the skills you need. There's good reason for this. You know the people who work for you and what to expect from them. They come without surprises — at least not too many — and most have proven their commitment and loyalty to your company. They deserve a first chance at any opportunity that will help them reach their potential and add to their pocketbooks. Loyalty and commitment are in short supply these days.

But sometimes the organization demands new talent. The person you need to fill a particularly important slot is not to be found among your current staff. There is simply no other choice; you must bring in the management you need from outside the company. You must hire an OUTSIDE PERSON! I capitalize because that's the way it will be said by many of your people, exclamation point and all.

Hiring a manager from outside the small company means change. You and your people know that a new person in a management role will have a strong impact on the organization. Adjustments will be necessary. In short, things will not stay the same. And while this may be exactly what you want, it is unlikely your people will greet the idea with enthusiasm, particularly those most directly affected.

Even the stoutest of employee hearts blanches at the hint of change. Change puts things at risk, rearranges comfortable patterns, and makes new demands. The best of us, fearless and forward-thinking though we may be, sniff at change with a wary, hesitant nose.

Business owners are, in this respect, not much different than the people who work for them. And change in the form of an OUTSIDE PERSON! is daunting. Owners, too, often speak that term in capitals, sensing that there's more than a kernel of truth in what Woodrow Wilson once said: "If you want to make enemies, try to change something." Not a cheerful thought when the last thing a business owner wants is to alienate or discourage employees. But if you can't find the skills you need in-house, you have no choice, you must hire from outside.

What are the risks?

For one thing, you might hire the wrong person. You may think that's not much of risk. After all, if he or she doesn't work out, you can always let the person go. True. But these days, that can be expensive, depending on your contract with the individual and local laws governing termination. The money issue is the least of it. Let's be honest, most of us take a long time deciding when a person should be terminated. We dither, justify, and rationalize until a lot of damage has been done, and if there is one thing a poorly selected manager brought in from the outside can do, it's damage. Nothing can upset systems, staff, and customers more than a new person in a position of authority. You must work hard to choose well.

Making judgments about our workers and colleagues is the toughest job there is. Not only are we vulnerable to being mislead or smoothly finessed, we can, in spite of our best efforts, simply make a bad call. And for the small business owner, the cost of such a mistake can be stressful and expensive.

Why all this negativity? Because if you're about to hire from outside to fill a position of authority, I want you to bring all of your considerable gray matter to bear on the decision and the selection process.

Start by considering the unique makeup of your company. What is its texture? How does it look, feel, act?

(a) What is the age group? Is everyone there under 25 or over 50?

(b) What systems are currently in place for information retrieval, employee suggestions, and the monitoring of production and sales?

(c) Will the systems provide objective data to assist you in monitoring the new person's performance?

(d) Is the attitude of the company rigid and formal or relaxed and informal?

(e) What is your company image? Cool and professional or busily casual?

(f) What are the philosophical and ethical principles under which you operate?

It isn't enough that an applicant have a 20-page resume with all the right skills; he or she must be right for your organization. Hold a clear picture of your corporate environment in your mind as you go through the hiring process, and ask yourself the following about each applicant.

(a) Will he or she fit into your organization?

(b) Will he or she be sensitive to your corporate universe?

(c) Will he or she bring new, necessary skills to the company?

(d) Did he or she ask questions beyond those related directly to the position available? About the company? Its people? Its history?

(e) Did he or she indicate an ability to listen and hear what you are saying?

(f) Do you feel he or she will accept and work under the ethical principles integral to your business?

While none of the above questions is easily quantifiable, each will help sensitize your instinctive reactions to the applicants. When all is said and done, when all the references are checked, your instinct about the person must be satisfied. You must feel good about your choice, and that means the person must fit your organization.

Don't hire a Harvard graduate because she is a Harvard graduate, or a high-profile image if you're a low-profile kind of company. You won't be happy and neither will the new employee. I'm not suggesting you hire a clone, but don't bring in an alien life-form either. Find a happy medium. It's your universe; protect it. Look for the basics first — I call them the must-haves: honesty, people skills, and common sense —

then look for the sauce. That master's degree from Harvard is a valuable bonus, but only if it comes with the right person.

A word about that background check. Do it! Thoroughly, exhaustively, and completely. Use every avenue you know to learn all you can about the person you intend to hire, and don't cut corners. Check, check, and check again.

Chapter Review

Your task is to provide an organization that facilitates and encourages measurement and reward of your employee's performance. Inherent in that structure must be the ability to monitor accountability. As a company grows, you need to know who's on first, who's on second, and how good a job each is doing — for the employee's sake as well as your own.

Good people are quick to realize there is no future in a company where expediency and excuses color the working day and the path to their future is a labyrinth of detours and dead ends. The clear, efficient organization of your company ensures an easier passage to success for both you and your employees.

- A practical company structure reduces error, frustration, and inequity.

- People deserve to know both their current place in the organization and their potential place.

- Job titles are communication tools; make them honest and accurate depictions of the position held.

- The company structure should encourage, not discourage, open communication.

- Managers hired from outside the company should be evaluated carefully and fit your corporate culture.

5
THE MAGIC CARPET

So much of what we call management consists in making it difficult for people to work.

Peter Drucker

One of the greatest inhibitors to small business growth is the inability of entrepreneurs to learn the fine art of delegation. Ensconced at the bridge, eyes on a distant star, they can slowly but surely sabotage the corporate ship. They share neither the wheel nor their vision, and they navigate with no crew.

To them delegation is a management buzzword, and they have no real sense of the strength it will bring to their organization or the power it has to shape the company's future. They don't understand that it is effective delegation that enables growing businesses to go the distance. Some may attempt it briefly, but let an employee falter or hesitate in the task assigned, and they jump in, reclaiming the wheel, power, and task in one convulsive movement. Others can't conceive of giving up one jot of control for even a moment.

Being in control is sensible. There's no argument with that. It is, after all, your business and your money at risk. Who's going to be the big loser if that account doesn't pay up or there has to be a quality recall on those widgets? You. It's wise not to forget it. Sure you occasionally get a little overworked, make the occasional mistake. Who doesn't? You're only human after all.

But if you absolutely must oversee every single detail of your operation, you are putting limits on what you can achieve and setting the stage for a dreary stagnation of wealth, talent and accomplishment. In fact, you will be lucky to even maintain the status quo for any useful length of time.

WHY DELEGATE?

Effective delegation opens up possibilities, and removes self-imposed roadblocks. Like the magic carpet in *The Arabian Nights*, it will take you "any place you wish. Nothing stands in its way, neither wall, nor tower, nor loftiest mountain. Tempests halt, doors fly open, such is its power."

Delegation is strong magic, but it is not mysterious. It is a learned skill and it is what separates the prosperous growing business from its stunted counterpart.

When people gather to work, they expect to be told what to do and how to do it, and they generally aim to do their best. Dealt with fairly and intelligently, they are an infinitely valuable resource. Given a chance, they will weave the first threads of your carpet. So loosen your grip and give them that chance. *Learn to trust, learn to share, learn to delegate.*

This does not mean dumping responsibility on untrained, unprepared employees, then standing back as they flounder and fail. It means standing with them — all the way.

WHAT ABOUT MISTAKES?

It's time you let someone else make a few mistakes. If that idea pulls you up short, I'm not surprised, but allowing someone else to make mistakes is part of the process of delegation. Before going any further, it's best you accept it will happen and work up the mental muscle to deal with it.

Does this mean you must tolerate incompetence, condone error, and approve ineptitude? Not at all. It means working with your subordinates to decrease the chance for mistakes while accepting their occasional failure in the same spirit as you accept your own. All it takes is one small shift in your attitude.

Let's assume you have a job to do and you do it wrong; you make a mistake. What do you do?

(a) You correct the error.

(b) You determine its cause.

(c) You take steps so it won't happen again.

The above actions are the logical, sequential behavior typifying effective problem-solving ability.

Now let's delegate the job to Gloria in accounting and see what happens when she makes the mistake. What do you do this time? Scream? Yell? Lay blame, huge and heavy, at poor Gloria's feet?

No. You do exactly what you did when the error was yours; shoulder the responsibility to find its cause and avoid its repetition. The work remains the same. Only this time you encourage Gloria to do it, while you monitor and support her efforts. By making this small shift in your thinking, you

Learn to delegate.

initiate a partnership approach to the problem. You both learn by Gloria's mistake.

Delegation is not abdication. You remain responsible for the decisions and actions affecting your enterprise, but with effective, thoughtful delegation you begin to share your power and take the first step from entrepreneur to manager.

NECESSARY TRAITS

What is delegation? In his book, *No-Nonsense Delegation,* Dale McConkey gives this definition: "Delegation is achievement of definite results by empowering and motivating subordinates to accomplish specific results for which the manager holds accountability."

It has not been said better. There are some potent words in that definition, clearly indicating that it takes a strong, goal-oriented person to do it well. It takes a leader willing to develop the attributes of sensitivity, a sense of fair play, and mental toughness.

1. Sensitivity

Your business is a hub of activities carried out by a diverse group of people, each with unique talents, dreams, and motivations. Through time, a culture has been created, a tiny universe with a unique and, perhaps, fragile identity. Empowering others to affect it more directly will challenge its flexibility. This is particularly true if you have been running your enterprise virtually single-handed. If you are considering bringing a manager in from outside the company, think long and hard. He or she must be equally sensitive to the special needs of your organization.

2. A sense of fair play

Without equity, that universe we just mentioned will implode. Delegation requires a just and very deft touch. Fairness allows a learning curve and gives credit where and to whom it is due. Fairness means rewarding the doers in your organization by giving them the chance to reach their potential. Being fair is one thing, but being perceived as fair is the real challenge. If you have two or three people ambitious for promotion and you can only choose one, it may seem impossible. But with this issue, your small company has a distinct advantage over its big brother. You can talk to people and so can your managers. There is no substitute for truth in management, and often simply taking the time to explain a decision is all it takes. If there is logic and goodwill behind it, employees will be supportive.

3. Mental toughness

Delegation takes mental toughness. Self-restraint is a good example — not jumping in, or on, your newly empowered manager because you *just know* you could do the job better and faster. You probably can. The question is, do you want to — forever? I've seen more than one business owner almost gloat when an employee fails at a given task. To them it validates their own importance, a perfect example of ego on overdrive. "See," they say. "Didn't I tell you that to get the job done, I have to do it myself?" Hear this phrase often enough and you have to know it's not the employee who's failed, it's the business owner.

Toughness also means straight, honest communication when it's called for. Given all your best efforts at training and selecting a manager, he or she may fail. In this case it's your job to consider the alternatives: reassignment, demotion, or termination. Then you must act quickly and decisively. Always a tough call — and always your call.

Is there an alternative to delegation in the small, growing company? Sure. Eighty-hour work weeks, stooped shoulders, frustrated, complaining employees, and wrinkles — yours. It's not a pretty sight.

WHAT TO DELEGATE

Do you have a firm understanding of what your job truly is? Have a look at Worksheet #3 in chapter 1. Back there, in question 19, we talked about where the buck stops and asked you to identify your primary responsibility. Review your answer.

I'm hoping you said something grand and high-minded about providing the leadership, guidance, and positive climate to ensure the economic performance of your company. You would be right if you did. That *is* your job: first, last, and always.

But you do a lot of things that drain power from your primary role. So, on Worksheet #10, let's get a clear picture of everything you do in an average month. Call it your task roster and make it as complete as possible. For now forget about the "Who best?" column. We'll get back to it.

You can't delegate every item on the list. That's impossible. Nor can you simply pawn off only the jobs that irritate and frustrate you. I suggest you analyze your tasks based on three criteria:

(a) Which tasks most often deter you from your primary responsibility of leadership and planning?

(b) What tasks are in conflict with, or overlap, other people's responsibilities?

(c) What tasks would be done more efficiently by another member of your organization?

By applying these three questions to your list, you will begin to see possibilities for effective delegation.

Now think about your people, review your organization chart, and go back and fill in the "Who best?" portion of the sheet.

As the chief executive officer, your organizational role is centered in leadership. Integral to this is motivating, developing, and guiding the people who have agreed to work for you. Equally important, you must give yourself the time to think, plan, and as much as you are able, anticipate the forces that

WORKSHEET #10
TASK ROSTER

Description of task	Hours	Who best?
_____	_____	_____
_____	_____	_____
_____	_____	_____
_____	_____	_____
_____	_____	_____
_____	_____	_____
_____	_____	_____
_____	_____	_____
_____	_____	_____
_____	_____	_____
_____	_____	_____
_____	_____	_____
_____	_____	_____
_____	_____	_____
_____	_____	_____
_____	_____	_____
_____	_____	_____
_____	_____	_____

will affect your company in the years to come. All tasks that detract from this activity should be ruthlessly examined and whenever possible be delegated.

In small companies, necessity often demands the sharing of tasks. Because you don't have the luxury of 15 people to back up each position, you cover for each other as and when it is needed. This is good — as far as it goes. But if it goes too far, and if, after years in business, you're still acting as receptionist every second Tuesday, you need to step back and rethink the situation. If the line between your work and a subordinate's is blurry, adjust your lenses and look hard. Review those job descriptions.

You've probably got jobs on your list that, due to lack of time or interest, you're giving short shrift. This type of task is easy to recognize because it's usually so low on your pecking order you need a backhoe to get to it. Examine it carefully, but first ask yourself if the job needs doing.

I know one business owner who, for reasons unfathomable, was compelled to keep an almost complete set of duplicate files on everything that went on in his office. His desk was a mountain of data he was obliged to regularly sort through and store. I don't like to think of the hours he spent keeping the mess organized, but he created the task and, in his mind at least, was stuck with it, stubbornly ignoring the fact that he was duplicating the work of his administrative staff.

If you've got a similar make-work project, get rid of it. Don't squander your most valuable, non-renewable resource — time — on useless activities.

HOW TO DELEGATE

It isn't every day you weave a magic carpet, so let's start with some basics. First, the choices. If you've completed your task list, make some selections from it. If you've already noted who's best to do the job, some of your work is done. But not all.

From the outset, your aim is to instill in your subordinate a desire to do the job and provide a definite sense of direction. To do this, your discussion with any employee should be purposeful and performance oriented.

If, until now, you alone have been doing the job, consider the job from the point of view of your subordinate. Other members of the staff who tend to defer easily and quickly to your requests may not be so forthcoming to your appointee. Make sure the mandate you give him or her is clearly communicated to all staff members, particularly those most concerned.

Don't simply provide a roster of duties to be performed. *Always discuss the why behind the job.* Place each task in its global setting. The greater the understanding each person has of his or her job, the greater contribution they can make. Give your chosen people every opportunity you can to excel — for their sake as well as yours.

Before assigning the responsibility, think deeply. On Worksheet #11, write it out clearly, examine it from all angles, and plan your follow-up.

Once you are completely satisfied with your definition of the job to be done, discuss it with your subordinate. Then listen.

No doubt the person being assigned the job will have his or her own opinions. If possible, incorporate them. When an employee invests something from his or her own experience bank, you are one step nearer to a job superlatively done. If the employee does suggest an improvement or a minor change, don't take it as a personal criticism on how you have been doing the job. So someone thinks he or she can do the job better than you. Maybe so. Isn't that exactly what you want?

WORKSHEET #11
DELEGATION CHECKLIST

The job is to _____

_____

What is its purpose? _____

_____

Priority? _____

What skills are required and why? _____

_____

_____

Why does the job need doing? _____

_____

When does it need to be completed? _____

Why does it have to be completed at that time?

_____

_____

What does the employee need to know to do the job?

_____

_____

_____

Access to support staff? _____

_____

_____

Feedback:

How often? _____

In what form? _____

Who needs to be informed? _____

_____

How do you intend to help? _____

_____

_____

Any training required? _____

_____

_____

Desired result? _____

_____

Method of follow-up? _____

_____

_____

_____

_____

_____

If employees express concern about their ability to do the job, listen, allay their fear where you can, and make a positive statement about your belief in them, but don't water down the mandate. Keep your purpose clear and your expectations high, and be certain to spell out the level of your assistance. Make it clear what form your support will take and under what conditions it is available. There is no sense in delegating if those whom you're entrusting with various tasks take up full-time residence in your office from that day forward. Don't cut them off, but do organize the communication process from the beginning.

At the end of a discussion in which you delegate tasks, ask the person these three questions or a variation thereof:

(a) Is there anything at all that you don't understand?

(b) Does the schedule look okay?

(c) Can you do it?

If the employee doesn't answer yes to all of them, be thankful he or she is honest, then start at the beginning and go over the job again.

BEWARE THE REBOUND

Delegation is not tennis with volleys and returns. In this game, you only serve once. The rule is when the job has been assigned properly it doesn't come back. Even the best employee is going to try — once. It works like this.

About a week or two into the job, Jim starts holding up your door supports. He's got a sheaf of paper in his hand. "Gotta minute?" he asks. You don't, but you say, "Sure, come in."

In he comes, frowning slightly. "Just a question or two about this procedures manual you want me to work up. I need Jayne's input by Tuesday, and it looks like she's going to be late — again." He manages a what-can-a-guy-do look and rolls his eyes for emphasis, then adds, "She's going to make mincemeat of your schedule on this."

"So? Tell her to hustle up," you say. "As I remember, the input from accounting is pretty much complete."

"That's what I thought too, but — well — you know Jayne." He shrugs and lifts a brow. "I told her you wanted it but —." Another shrug.

"Leave it with me, I'll speak to her."

STOP!

You just received an inside lob. Getting the input from Jayne is Jim's job, remember? Make sure he keeps it — all of it. If he has a serious problem completing the task, schedule a meeting where it can be discussed in depth. Don't let the standards you set for Jim be eroded by your random interventions. Stay accessible, sure, but stay disciplined. If you take part of the job back, chances are you'll end up with the whole thing.

So every time you're tempted to use the phrase, "Leave it with me," or that other no-no, "I'll take care of it," think again.

What should you have said when Jim started to unload his problem on your plate? How about something like this: "Yes, Jayne's pretty overloaded right now. Why not remind her again about the importance of the schedule, which by the way is ours not mine, if I remember right. Oh, and you might try Chris in admin, they have at least some of what you need on file. If not, let Jayne know her department's the only one lagging. She won't like that. You'll think of something, Jim. Let me know the results — say — in two days."

In the above instance the task stays solidly where it belongs — with Jim. You did your job by being accessible, making a couple of positive suggestions, and asking for results within a specified period of time.

FOLLOW-UP

Remember, delegation is not abdication. You are accountable for the results achieved (or not achieved) by your subordinates. Because of that you need to monitor and measure their work. It may be as simple as asking for a brief get-together every Wednesday morning to a formal request for a written report to be on your desk at 10 a.m. every Monday. It's your choice.

The main thing is to have a method of monitoring that both you and your subordinate feel comfortable with. If you haven't followed any rigid reporting procedures to this date, you may want to stay with an informal approach, although I strongly recommend you request some form of written report. Even a brief update in the form of a memo will clarify and simplify the follow-up procedure.

Enter times and dates for follow-up activity in your diary on the day the tasks are assigned, and when you do meet to discuss your subordinate's work, give it, and him or her, your full attention and your support.

Follow-up, defined as "action to increase the effectiveness of previous action," is crucial to getting the results you want from the delegation process. Like Nike says, "Just do it."

LEAVE YOUR EGO AT HOME

Unwittingly, and to our detriment, we humans often go to great lengths to protect a fragile ego or feed a demanding one. Both can manifest themselves in similar behavior: a need to take charge, to prove ourselves over and over again, to bask in the spotlight, and to seize credit wherever and whenever credit is available for the taking. Such an attitude obstructs the process of delegation.

While a strong, healthy ego provides the emotional toughness to make us leaders, an unhealthy, greedy one turns us into bosses employees love to hate. It's my guess that unbalanced, undisciplined egos have destroyed more businesses than all the depressions and recessions combined.

By all means, build your self-esteem with quiet pride from a job well done, believe in yourself when no one else does, give yourself a pat on the back when it's well and truly earned. But when it comes to the avaricious, gluttonous ego — ice it. You'll be doing yourself and your organization a great kindness.

If you find the act of delegating authority and tasks difficult, ask yourself some hard questions about why it isn't working. Run an ego check; you could be your own worst enemy.

Chapter Review

Delegation takes a full and genuine commitment on your part if it is to work. It isn't easy to let go, to let others do what you have done so very, very well. But if you are to grow, it is as necessary as a baby's first stumbling step.

Too many business owners never take that step and they see their businesses languish or silently slip into the backwater. They steadfastly maintain control over the most mundane daily chores. They work long. They work hard. They work alone. And they miss out on the unmeasurable satisfaction of helping others grow, learn, and achieve both as employees and people. Don't you. Begin now to weave your magic carpet.

- The ability to delegate is the key to business growth.
- Fear of mistakes is not a valid reason to avoid delegation.
- Delegation is not abdication.
- When the task is assigned, don't take it back.
- After delegation: support, monitor, and follow up.
- Don't let your ego sabotage the delegation process.

6
INFORMATION, PLEASE

Get your facts first, then you can distort 'em as you please.

Mark Twain

Smart business owners are good detectives. They have an insatiable need to know about everything that has an impact on their organization. It is a need that sets them on, and keeps them on, a quest to gather external and internal information on a regular basis. They are curious, observant, and attentive to detail: methodical in building a factual framework for sometimes complex decision making.

They don't make decisions in a vacuum. They ask questions of themselves and employees to constantly monitor what affect growth and change are having on the company, its people, and customers. When they can no longer draw valid conclusions about the state of the business by walking the shipping floor, they are quick to fill the gap by instituting systems to provide reliable, meaningful information. They become adept at accumulating, analyzing, filtering, and selecting useful information to affirm their assumptions and support their decisions. In short, they stay informed.

INSTINCTIVE UNDERSTANDING

Instinctive understanding is another way of saying "gut feel." There isn't anyone in business who doesn't revere this mystic phenomenon and recognize its part in their success. Often it is the sole propellant to get into business in the first place. You just *feel* the time is right, the product is right, and that you have a good chance for success. When you ultimately succeed, you tend to put a high degree of trust in the nebulous power of your particular gut feeling. As you should. Anyone who tells you to turn a deaf ear to your intuitive voice is doing you a disservice.

Good instincts are important to the success of your business, but they're mysterious, fickle things and they don't always show up when you need them. As a factor in your decision-making process, they are invaluable, but as the business grows, instinct alone is not enough. You need backup. That backup is hard facts and current information about all aspects of your business.

In his book, *What They Don't Teach You at Harvard Business School*, Mark J. McCormack puts it this way: "You can't take an edge until you have first taken a look at the facts. Facts

Smart business owners are good detectives.

alone won't guarantee you an edge, but they can protect you from handing it over to someone else."

If you stumble around the marketplace unobservant and uninformed, the only edge you're likely to happen across will be dangerously precipitous. Learn to ground that remarkable intuition of yours in a base of hard, factual information. The source for information can be either internal or external.

INTERNAL INFORMATION

1. Information overload

Every day, reams of paper are used by companies across North America; facts and figures festoon each and every sheet of it. Computers everywhere are doing their job. Groaning and droning, they churn out data: financial reports, pro formas, budgets, sales figures, analysis, more analysis, analysis of the analysis.

There is no shortage of information. But finding the right data in a small, active business can be like seeking diamonds in the sand. Why? Because most owner managers haven't taken the time to identify the information they need and want. They haven't given the information-gathering activity within their company the priority it deserves. Even the basics are often ignored. Financial statements are constantly late, or wrong, or both. Historical data is coffee stained, sporadic, and misfiled. Or, worse yet, owners stoutly maintain that everything they need to know is in their heads.

If your tendency is to regard information gathering as a distant cousin of woolgathering, think again. Organized information is integral to the professionally run business. Not only is it an essential component in decision making, it is a management tool that insurers, banks, and sophisticated investors expect you to use wisely and well. If you look to the future, to the day when you may want to sell or merge your business, you'll find that information, current and historical, is fundamental to establishing price and terms. There isn't a buyer in the world willing to trust that head of yours or those incomplete files you've dragged from the storage room. They will want an accumulation of hard, accurate data, and it will be in your interest to provide it.

You'll be smart to accept the following maxims and plan accordingly.

(a) Information is important. You and your subordinates should be working from a base of factual, current data at all times.

(b) Information needs to be managed. Information must be treated as the critical resource it is. It must be monitored, controlled, reviewed, and its relevance evaluated on a consistent schedule.

(c) Information needs definition. You must decide on and identify the information you need. It should be shaped to meet your needs.

(d) Information should be accurate. Be unrelentingly right! Do not condone or accept substandard information. It's useless.

(e) Information should be current. Retrieve information from as close to its source as you can get and as quickly as you can. Push yourself and your subordinates to make and meet information deadlines.

Your business is just that — *your* business. It has a pulse and heartbeat all its own. It takes expertise to monitor its beat.

Instant, accurate information is an enormous advantage. Think about it.

Let's assume you hook your enterprise up to a business cardiogram. You create a graphic record of your business heartbeat, a picture of activity at the moment it occurs. At any irregularity on the graph, any small deviation from the norm, you can react with stunning speed. If the deviation is enough to threaten the health of your business, your immediate response may save the day.

Compare this approach to that of many small business owners who work with either no information or data so ancient it's one tottering step from the archives. When the situation is critical, and with no accurate data to draw on, that gut feeling of theirs will probably only be the early warning signal for an ulcer.

Today's business moves at a rapid pace. To keep up, to be at the ready, you need warm-blooded, lively information as current and timely as the morning newscast. While you may not be able to monitor it nanosecond by nanosecond, you can strive for the freshest, most precise information available to you.

2. What you need to know

Think of your business as having two kinds of information: concrete and abstract. Concrete information is numbers. They are hard and conclusive — what you see is what you get — because it's the history of what you've done. For most businesses, the following categories are typical: profits, losses, revenues, loan amounts, payroll, payables, receivables, bank balances, bad debts, production and sales statistics, etc.

Abstract information is everything else, soft information that requires subtle interpretation and response. It is mainly the result of people activity. For example:

(a) The sales division is complaining about commissions.

(b) Due to the increased work load, a position has opened up for an assistant supervisor in production.

(c) Your main competitor underbid you on that last contract by 20%.

At one time or another during the month, information much like the above crosses your desk. While the abstract data probably comes to you verbally, the concrete data, the numbers that tell your business story, should come packaged in a form designed for easy assimilation. Let's look at those numbers.

Chances are, you scan the concrete information, seeking out totals, summaries, and bottom lines. If you're like many small business owners, you first say a small prayer that the figures are accurate this month. When the numbers tilt in your favor, you smile. If not, you get the bottom-line blues. You delve deeper into the numbers looking for clues for what went wrong. You look for areas to improve and make changes. You make plans. The more current the information, the more valuable it is. One thing you can't do is affect the information one way or another. You've heard it before — you can't change history. You can only learn from it.

Hard and soft data is linked. Look back at the examples under abstract information. In every case, action is required either by you or one of your subordinates; decisions need to be made. What do you base them on? Gut feel? Facts? Gut feel and facts? Select your own options, but in most cases those decisions would be facilitated by some hard, cold facts.

It takes a special effort on the part of the owner-manager to develop and maintain a path of ready access to pertinent, current data and even more to streamline the data into a form that is productive and useful. You need to treat information in the same organized way you treat the deluge of paper that inundates you on a daily basis.

Think about it. Do you read every line of junk mail as well as all of those trade magazines and newspapers that litter your desk? Of course you don't. It would be a ridiculous waste of time and you know it. But you also know that there is worthwhile data buried among the dross. So, you scan, absorb what's urgent, file what you think is necessary and discard the rest.

Learn to do the same with the mountain of paper your computer generates. Practice the art of distillation. Dig into it until you find the numbers you want and summarize. Develop a reporting system that is easily accessible. Extract and reduce until you have the essence of your business at your fingertips and file the rest.

Businesses generate numbers at a staggering rate, and each small business has a unique set of numbers that tells its story. Some are what I call workhorse numbers. Produced in a timely fashion, these both inform and contribute to a more proactive management style. Here are a couple of examples:

(a) The company that sells time (i.e., consultants, services) might find it useful to tally time sheets daily, not only to keep an eye on billable versus non-billable hours, but to enable them to submit invoices the moment the job is complete. The sooner that invoice goes out, the sooner the cash comes in.

(b) The company that manufactures widgets may find it useful to watch production statistics more closely. Spotting a production problem early could allow time to make critical improvements.

Other numbers are indicators or ratios gleaned from your financial history; they work as a data base for long-term decision making and planning. They originate from analysis:

(a) Sales analysis: identifying peaks and valleys by comparing one year to another, one month to another.

(b) Expense analysis: what you are spending, where and on what.

(c) Margin analysis: monitoring the difference between the cost and sale price of your goods or service.

(d) Balance sheet ratios: assets to liabilities, liquidity.

(e) Statistics analysis, all kinds: production and sales reports, personnel reports, inventory records.

Such analyses are done by professionals on a routine basis. Like arrows, they point out inefficiencies, inconsistencies, and

85

the relative quality of existing information systems. See the appendix for basic ratio calculations.

There are some numbers singled out by small business owners that make no sense at all to the outsider. I know one business owner who swore he could estimate his entire month's revenue on the sale of one particular part. It's the same logic used in an election year when they predict, "As Maine goes, so goes the nation." In his mind, that number told him what he wanted to know, so he tracked it. Fortunately, he paid equal attention to the more rational outpourings of his computer department.

On the following three worksheets (Worksheets #12, #13, and #14), start to analyze your specific information needs. Think about the following

- What information do you need?
- Is it currently available?
- Where is it?
- What form should it take?
- Who can provide it?

Defining what you need to know takes work. In the beginning, you may need to wade through the extraneous to the pertinent. Take a look at these worksheets, jot down some notes, and make a start.

These worksheets cover the three main divisions of most businesses — financial, marketing, and production — but customize them if you need to. Start by reviewing the information you now receive and work from there.

Remember, your aim is to gather only the information you need and not one digit more. An efficient filing system ensures the balance of the data is there if and when you want it. For now you want only the essentials and you want them pronto.

WORKSHEET #12
FINANCIAL INFORMATION NEEDS

List financial information you currently receive and when.

Description of Data   Date Received

_____   _____

_____   _____

_____   _____

_____   _____

_____   _____

Do you receive too much data?   Yes _____   No _____

Do you receive it on time?   Yes _____   No _____

List information you want and when you want it.

_____   _____

_____   _____

_____   _____

_____   _____

Outline the most effective format: (Look for the summaries, comparisons, totals, percentages, bottom lines. Remember — reduce and extract!)

_____

_____

_____

_____

_____

WORKSHEET #13
MARKETING INFORMATION NEEDS

List marketing information you currently receive and when.

Description of Data   Date Received

_____   _____

_____   _____

_____   _____

_____   _____

_____   _____

Do you receive too much data?   Yes _____   No _____

Do you receive it on time?   Yes _____   No _____

List information you want and when you want it.

_____   _____

_____   _____

_____   _____

_____   _____

Outline the most effective format: (Look for the summaries, comparisons, totals, percentages, bottom lines. Remember — reduce and extract!)

_____

_____

_____

_____

_____

WORKSHEET #14
PRODUCTION INFORMATION NEEDS

List production information you currently receive and when.

Description of Data   Date Received

_____   _____

_____   _____

_____   _____

_____   _____

_____   _____

Do you receive too much data?   Yes _____   No _____

Do you receive it on time?   Yes _____   No _____

List information you want and when you want it.

_____   _____

_____   _____

_____   _____

_____   _____

Outline the most effective format: (Look for the summaries, comparisons, totals, percentages, bottom lines. Remember — reduce and extract!)

_____

_____

_____

_____

_____

Lest you believe for a moment I am encouraging you to be a wide brush and pay no attention to the intricacies of your enterprise, think again. No small business owner can run his or her business solely by using broad strokes and paying no attention to detail. What you must do is avoid *useless* detail. You have a growing business to run and that means forward thinking, planning, and organizing for coming growth. Working with the right information, rather than excessive information, frees your time to do just that.

So get the facts you need fast and file the rest. They'll be there when you need them.

EXTERNAL INFORMATION

Thinking about opening another outlet? Need market data? Considering importing? Exporting? Bidding on government work? Planning a new product line? Need to know the labor force in Mondragone? Consumer spending trends? Demographic information? It's all there, anything you want to know, when you want to know it. Try a little digging.

1. Libraries

The first place to look is the library. The public library holds a world of information, but there are also academic, community college, historical, newspaper, and company libraries. If you need a specific type of library, consult a library directory.

If your needs are simple (e.g., basic statistics or historical data), you may only need to consult directories, almanacs, encyclopedias, dictionaries, and general reference books. If your need is for in-depth information, you may have to tap periodicals, specialized reference books, government documents, original material (private papers, public records, etc.), experts, and organizations. There is usually too much information; rarely is there too little. Here are a few tips for dealing with it.

(a) Don't judge a book by its cover; books always have more information than a title is able to suggest.

(b) Study the table of contents so you can zoom in on the information you need as well as making sure you don't miss something important.

(c) One book is not enough. Carry your limit out of the library and then set aside those you don't need.

(d) Don't believe everything you read. Try to recognize biases that may taint information.

(e) Know when to stop and don't waste time once you have what you need.

(f) Don't rule out luck; hunches can be useful. Above all else, know when, where, and how to ask for help.

A word here about librarians. I never met one I didn't like. They are helpful, informed, and absolute geniuses when it comes to finding the exact piece of information you need, no matter how illusive or bizarre. They are your passport to the information you need. Remember too, you can contact a library by phone. Some libraries even have special staff to handle enigmatic time-consuming questions.

2. Clipping services

Some of the most important information sources to a business person are current. One such source is magazines or periodicals. There are hundreds of popular magazines that report on politics, economics, and other concerns, but there are thousands of scholarly and specialty magazines that provide in-depth looks into given subjects. They help you find experts as well as notice trends and developments before they are reported in popular magazines, on television, or in newspapers.

The key to these periodicals is the indexes found at the library. Go there and have a look at what's available. It's unlikely you will want to order all of them, but if truly pertinent information from any of them would be a benefit, you can subscribe to a clipping service. Clipping services are efficient information sources because they collect articles and arrange them by subject. They are real time savers, but such services can be costly. Whether they are worth the price to you will depend on your needs.

3. Statistics

Originating from universities and colleges, private organizations, government, and industry, statistics are published in articles, books, reports, dissertations, and statistical yearbooks and directories. Again, indexes at your library are the key to locating the local, regional, national, or international statistics you may need. The library will also have a variety of statistical yearbooks from professional and trade associations.

4. Computer data bases

Far and away the star of the information age is the computer. Our electronic allies play a major role in information gathering; much of the information already mentioned is available by computer. There are now thousands of data bases available to the public from hundreds of suppliers, and often the information is more current than in the printed counterparts. If it's not your idea of a good time to sit at a keyboard, try a computer search firm. Remember, if you want some information hot off the disk, define your need clearly and set parameters. This saves time and time is....

5. Other sources

Information centers are everywhere. Government agencies, consulates and embassies, chambers of commerce, and trade and professional associations frequently handle requests for information. If they can't help you, they'll often direct you to an appropriate source. Above all else, presume the information you need exists, because it probably does.

Chapter Review

Information — of all kinds — is a powerful contributor to the growth of your enterprise. Don't let it overwhelm you or let the sheer abundance of it deter you from digging in and taking what you need.

- Stay informed, observant, and curious, and seek information.

- Gut instinct is *a* component, not *the* component in effective decision making.

- Use current, reliable, timely information to fortify your decisions, both internal and external.

- Distill your information; leave behind the excess and extract the truly significant.

- Standard financial ratios provide objective feedback on the performance of your business.

7

YOUR BUSINESS FAMILY

If you cannot get rid of the family skeleton, you may as well make it dance.

George Bernard Shaw

Prediction. You're not going to be in business very long before you tangle with the issue of family — either real or corporate.

It could be when near and dear relatives start to view your business as a one-stop job opportunity for every family member between here and Tulsa. Or it could be when your business family starts to creak and groan under the pressure of too much change and growth.

Both families demand care and attention, and as neither comes with a guarantee it will always act for the greater good (the greater good in this case being your company), you have your work cut out for you.

THAT FAMILY FEELING

"We're just like family here."

You've heard the expression, haven't you? Most likely from your own long-term employees. It's often used to describe the familial atmosphere of a new business. It implies nurturing, warmth, caring, and a host of other solicitous feelings that contribute to a "people-first" working environment.

Yes, one big happy family, until the business grows and adjustments are demanded of its members. You soon discover adaptability is not a family trait. About this time, the self-defined family tends to look a bit glum.

94

There's a new kid on the block: change.

Well-run start-up companies often invoke a family feeling among employees in the early days. While you may not deliberately set out to create this feeling, it can and often does create itself. More than once, I've heard people say they feel closer to the people they work with than their real family. Certainly they spend more time with them.

The easy familiarity most of us associate with family is inevitable where people must depend on each other and work together in close quarters — often for long hours. They become involved in each other's lives, both at and away from work. The sense of family grows as people communicate more intimately and learn to accommodate each other's strengths and weaknesses. Through time, they develop a sincere concern for each other's welfare, and like family, what affects one affects the other. When that family is threatened, from within or without, they circle the wagons.

A big contributor to this comforting familiarity is access to the "head of the family." They can talk to you, directly to you, whenever they want. There is a strong sense of being in on things and near the top. When they speak out, they are heard. As individuals, they have the satisfaction of having a direct impact on the plans and decisions giving shape to their working lives. Often, this is simply the result of close proximity to you and your open office door. No matter what the reason, in the first days of the business, that family feeling works for them, you, and the good of the company.

In the wake of growth, all of that is at risk. It is tested when the growth of the business demands more structure, altered reporting lines, new and updated procedures, or the hiring of new people. It must also withstand the changes you make to your own work habits. It becomes more difficult for you to keep your door permanently open, to maintain direct accessibility. Certain decisions now require confidentiality, either by agreement or common sense, and sharing every detail of the business is no longer feasible. In the eyes of your people, you've gone from being friendly Joe or Mary to Bigshot Exec in the corner office, if not literally, at least figuratively. Things are changing, and within the self-defined family the status quo is threatened. Feelings are hurt, the grapevine hums, criticisms emerge, morale hits bottom. The happy family is in domestic meltdown.

Avoid this scenario by accepting that change, especially rapid change, causes stress. It makes people nervous about their place in the scheme of things and fills them with questions. The smartest thing you can do is anticipate this response and head it off before stress becomes *dis*tress.

Consider a west-coast T-shirt design and manufacturing company. We'll call the president, Sarah. For Sarah, the hard work and talent of her sharp, fashion-conscious staff really paid off. They came up with an environmental theme and a couple of slogans that became very hot sellers. The orders poured in and the bottom-line bounced. Then they needed more space, more staff, more everything. Sarah had always worked hard and now she worked harder. She spent hours behind her closed office door, frantically trying to keep up with the changes affecting her company. Some days it seemed that all she did was go from one meeting to another. It wasn't at all like before when she had time to talk to people, linger awhile in cutting, or have a cup of coffee with the sales staff.

To her, the closed doors and the endless meetings were an attempt to plan and organize for the company's growth. To the staff, Sarah's changed working pattern merely meant she was unavailable — and maybe getting just a little bit full of herself. They didn't like it. They were used to the head of the family being accessible. The change was unwelcome and suspect.

It was an outspoken supervisor who finally brought the feelings of the disgruntled staff to a surprised Sarah's attention. Sarah had been completely unaware that an alteration in her working behavior could so affect the staff's attitude to her and the company. She never short-changed them on information again. And she didn't forget to thank the supervisor.

That family feeling need not be sacrificed simply because your business is a little bigger and your time is a little shorter. It's too powerful a force to abandon so offhandedly. Hang on to it — forever if you can. Your business family need not be a shortsighted, self-protective unit that cowers at the unknown. With some effort on your part, it can be made stronger and more resilient.

Walk a step or two in your employees' shoes, try to see things from their point of view, and give them all the information necessary to allay fears and avoid misconceptions. Keeping the grapevine filled with good, solid information is one step on the way to domestic harmony.

Think about the changes your small business has undergone so far and think ahead. Ask yourself these questions:

(a) What changes do I plan or expect in the near future?

(b) Who will be affected, directly or indirectly?

(c) What information do I need to share?

Don't be a company of plots, schemes, and secrets. The grapevine exposes most of them anyway, usually with an unwelcome twist. When there is a need for confidentiality or the occasional closed door, explain why. But, in general, operate in as open and as forthright a manner as you can.

Be consistent in informing your people of the events and plans that will affect them and their working relationships. Be sensitive to that basic trait all intelligent human creatures share — curiosity — and make it work for, not against, the interests of the company.

To keep that family feeling, the rule is *communicate*.

PEOPLE WHO DON'T GROW WITH THE COMPANY

I can see you nodding. You have employees like this. Right? Some are good, hardworking people who have been with you since the beginning. In those early days, they were with you all the way, giving extra hours, weekends, whatever was necessary to get the job done. Close at the time, you worked shoulder to shoulder. That was then.

Now? They're no longer up to the tasks at hand. They're still working hard. They're still loyal and willing, but for unfathomable reasons, they are now your lowest producers, poorest supervisors, or most ineffective managers. You have an unpleasant twinge telling you that you should do something about it. But you owe them and your debt stops you cold.

There's another type. The employees who think because they have been with you since the beginning, maybe put in a few of those long hours, they are now entitled to rest comfortably on their long-dry laurels and let others do the work. What work they do, they do grudgingly, certain they are meant for better things. They are quick to let you know they are due for promotion and expect it at the first opportunity. Their approach is forthright. "I've done a lot for this company," they tell you. You can't deny it. They have.

You also can't deny you'd be better off installing a bust of Napoleon in that coveted corner office than employees like this. It would be equally as effective and a lot less trouble. Still, you say to yourself, they have been with you a long time — maybe you do owe them.

It doesn't matter if a person does his or her incompetent best with a smile or without, the result is the same substandard work. You must take action.

It is difficult, if not impossible, to be cool and objective when emotions are engaged. Most successful owners are fully invested in their small enterprises. The investment is more than cash and collateral; it's a moral and emotional commitment that builds loyalty, mutual respect, and fosters a unique kinship with the organization's people. As business owners, we have no desire to cause unhappiness or financial distress to our people. Add to that the fact that most of us are masters of confrontation avoidance and you have the seeds for procrastination and denial on a major scale. When it comes to dealing with difficult employees we are, to put it simply, wimps.

Sorry, the problem won't go away. If you think you can outwait it, that old Bob is just going to quit one of these days to make your job easier, think again. The chances are better that Bob knows a good thing when he sees it. From his perspective, seniority, coupled with the boss's undying gratitude for that unpaid overtime a year or two ago, translates into comfortable job security. Bob is in for the long haul. He has got it made; you've got a management dilemma.

Your job is to protect the company's future for yourself and all the hardworking employees who depend on it. Incompetence in any form threatens that future. But let's not get overly dramatic. I'm not saying that Bob, single-handedly, will destroy the business. At issue here is not the hapless Bob's inability to do his job. No. It's your ability to tolerate it and pave the way for more of the same that is the real cause for concern. Equity in the work place is paramount. If reliable, good work is expected from others, it must be expected from Bob.

You know that's how it must work. Eisenhower said once, "Nothing is easy in war. Mistakes are always paid for in casualties and troops are quick to sense any blunder made by their commanders."

To ignore Bob's ineptitude for any longer than it takes you to figure out a way to handle it is a mistake. You do have an obligation to Bob: not to give him pay increases he doesn't deserve, not to close your eyes to his poor work, and certainly not to guarantee him lifetime employment. You owe him straight-up talk, a good, hard listen, and a chance to set things right. How do you do it? As a first effort, try the method outlined below.

First, examine your options:

(a) Demotion

(b) Reassignment

(c) Termination

(d) Another chance

(e) Other (select one and a backup):

_____

_____

Then straighten your shoulders and face Bob. Discuss his poor performance; explain why it can't be allowed to continue, putting it squarely in the context of the organization as a whole. Praise past contributions but quickly move to the here and now — and the future. Be direct, honest, and make a genuine effort to find a solution. Assume he wants this, too. Try to put aside preconceived ideas about why his quality of work is poor. Listen. Then listen again. Be open to the possibility the situation can be rectified. If you can help, do it. Tell him exactly what your expectations are. You want to be as sure as you can that Bob gets a good shot at improving.

By being candid and forthcoming, you've done your job. From here on in, it's up to Bob. If in a few days, a week, a month, you see nothing has changed, start at the top of the list. But remember, there are only so many chances for any of us.

FAMILY TIES

What about including *real* family members in the business? There are few small businesses that haven't got a story to tell about mixing business and family. Conventional wisdom, which the dictionary defines as prudence, says don't do it. That's probably good advice, and you can no doubt go along with it until your favorite nephew needs a job to pay for college, your brother loses his middle-management position at the local bank and tells you he'd make one heck of a controller for your growing enterprise, or your Great-Aunt Celia bails you out from a financial tight spot in exchange for shares and a vice-presidency.

There is an old Italian proverb that says, "The rich never have to seek out their relatives." Ditto the small business owner. The truth is, family and business do mix — frequently with unpredictable, but not always adverse, results. There can be benefits in working with trustworthy, industrious family members.

(a) They're supportive even when times get tough. They may even offer to take a pay cut to help you out. I've heard more than one business owner talk about their gratitude and debt to a selfless family member.

There are few small businesses that haven't got a story to tell about mixing business and family.

(b) They know you well enough to be truthful — even when it hurts. Truth is always a priceless gift. There are times when only a relative has the courage to say the words, "You're wrong."

(c) You don't have to be boss all the time. Caring family understand and accept your doubts and insecurities without judgment or condemnation. They can be a handy sounding board when you need to speak without measuring every word.

The family and business mix gets dicey when you allow a relative to join your company full of illusions and confusions about what is expected of him or her on the job. When a family member believes he or she is under your protection or has guaranteed tenure, trouble is the certain outcome. If you think it's difficult to terminate a regular employee, you haven't yet faced firing your favorite nephew or Great-Aunt Celia. When hiring any member of your family, approach it with all the honesty and professionalism you can muster. You owe it to him or her, and more important, you owe it to all the other employees in the organization.

We've come a long way from hereditary aristocracy, where bloodline and kinship were the prerequisites to opportunity of any kind, where family ties, and only family ties, determined the shape of our future. The only heritage that counts now is a democratic one. Our North American unease about hiring relatives is rooted deeply in our democratic principles. We are reluctant nepotists, and that is as it should be. Blatant patronage and favoritism have no place in your company.

But while you'd prefer not to hire your brother, you're probably going to do it anyway. Why? Because there's a chance he can do the job, because he is in need, and because he's your brother. You can't turn your back on him. But you can take steps that will help him fit in and do his job. It starts with communication and ends, if you are successful, with understanding. This discussion is essential prior to employment. Once he's on the job, it's too late.

(a) Discuss your concerns about hiring him, who in the organization it will have direct impact on, and why.

(b) Talk to him about your people — their loyalty, their contribution to the company, their expectations. Give him a true feeling for the existing corporate family.

(c) Outline and explain the company structure and its management goals and tell him who does what.

(d) Sensitize him to the concerns of others in your organization. Prepare him to deal intelligently with some distrust and resistance.

(e) Accurately and completely describe his job and his reporting line. Be detailed.

(f) Tell him your expectations of him will be high, and that to prove himself to you and his working peers, he must be prepared to work hard — perhaps extra hard.

(g) Advise him he will be judged on the basis of his effort and the results of those efforts while on the job.

(h) Make it clear that if he views the job as a favor, it's the last one you're prepared to give and that you will terminate him if he proves incapable of the job.

(i) Make it clear there is no back door, side door, or trap door that leads to your office. He must at all times use the regular channels of reporting and communication. (And so must you!)

Of all the points above, asking a family member to work harder than the next person may seem unfair. But he or she should see it is a small price to pay for jumping the line. He or she will be scrutinized and more *will* be expected; he or she would be smart to accept it and act accordingly for both your sakes.

Having said all this, put that relative on the payroll. Give him or her a chance to earn the respect of coworkers, then let the results speak for themselves.

No doubt when you tell your people you are hiring your brother, a few eyebrows will lift, but if you haven't trodden on a dozen work-weary toes, or demoted worthy Mary to make a place for him, most people will give you and him the benefit of the doubt.

The rule is, if the family member you hire fails to do what is expected of him or her, take action.

Chapter Review

As a business owner, you are asking your employees, related or otherwise, to be responsible, hardworking, and dependable. No doubt you are quick to recognize when one of them lets the "family" down or doesn't live up to your own behavior. Keep the information flowing and the dialogue frank.

- Accept that change can cause stress.
- Maintain accessibility.
- Keep your business family informed.
- Be conscious of changes in your behavior.
- Don't try to outwait a problem with an employee.
- Lay the ground rules early if you hire a relative.
- Expect the same performance (or better) from a family member as you would from any employee.

8
TRAPS AND HAZARDS

Experience keeps a dear school, but fools will learn in no other.

Benjamin Franklin

You are not the Adam or Eve of the entrepreneurial world. Thousands — millions — have gone before. Through trial, error, and painful firsthand experience, lessons were learned. Those lessons are available to you. All you have to do is look and listen, then carefully consider how to use what you learn to make your path smoother. It makes sense to learn what we can from the scars of others.

A small business is more than columns of figures on a computer printout, it's more than a minuscule contributor to the GNP, and it's certainly more than a record in that big tax computer in the sky. Your business is a slice of time each day when people come together and, if you're lucky, try to work for a shared goal. The reasons people show up at all are as diverse and intriguing as they are.

Some have no where else to go.

Some want a paycheck every week.

Some want a paycheck until they have enough points to quit and live off insurance.

Some work because they want to, some because they need to, and some because society — or their mate — says they must.

And while some would rather work for you than anyone else, others would rather work for anyone else but you. You probably can't tell the difference.

We've all heard a business described as a vehicle for making money. That's a fair description, appropriate for you and your people. The business supports all of you. But, as a vehicle, it's a wobbly, teetering conveyance at best, and there are rough patches along the way.

Let's look at some of the things that can, when not handled properly, cause dangerous vibrations.

THE SMUDGED LENS

Somewhere on your way to corporate greatness, if you're not careful, your vision can blur. When things are going well, when a business is growing, you may feel all-powerful, invincible. Unconsciously, you can slip into muddy thinking, and muddy thinking can lead to deep and dangerous waters.

We've all seen small businesses make the mistake of assuming the first stage of growth is a permanent condition and in the rosy glow of early success lower their guard. Their reactions to growth-related changes in their organization are not always positive and certainly not always rational. These are the signs:

(a) Their thinking narrows. They internalize, believing that nothing is important except what is going on within the four walls housing the enterprise. They ignore the voices of the market, the economy, and the activities of their competitors.

(b) They spend inordinate amounts of time in meetings dealing with policies, procedures, and personalities. Plans become inflated and grandiose.

(c) They make rules and regulations instead of sales. They like to make terse, abrupt signs that tell customers what they will and won't do.

(d) They start to take their customers for granted. They charge more and give less value.

(e) They see customers as unreasonable intrusions into their corporate peace, or, worse yet, as inconvenient necessities.

(f) They make arbitrary, genuinely stupid decisions out of pride and puffery and delude themselves into thinking they're acting for the good of the business.

(g) They suffer from delusions and convince themselves the good times will roll forever. They're dynamite managers, omnipotent and in control. They can do no wrong.

(h) They distance themselves from the basic action of the business and from their people.

(i) They spend the business's cash with the glee and abandon of lottery winners rather than with the prudence of experienced businesspeople.

So when you find yourself feeling satisfied or a touch smug, it's time for a reality check. Clean your lenses. See first-stage growth in your small company as a stepping stone, not the end of the rainbow. Meditate on its effect on your way of thinking and your decision making. And while you're about it, think about this Joel Chandler Harris saying: "Watch out when you're getting all you want. Fattening hogs ain't in luck."

Turn to Worksheet #15 and answer a few questions. While many of them can be answered with a simple yes or no, go past that. Make notes. Jot down some ideas and think about how you are handling your initial success. Doing this exercise is good for your business and even better for you.

Early success, though undeniably sweet, can be dangerous to the long-time health of your business. If you don't keep a cool head and clear vision, it's all too easy to lose sight of

WORKSHEET #15
CLEANING THE LENS

Do you believe in resting on your laurels? Are you? Are others? _____

_____

_____

_____

Are you as concerned with the whole business as you were in the beginning? Is your thinking as broad as it was?

_____

_____

_____

Are you still marketing hard and creatively? When did you last use a fresh approach? _____

_____

_____

_____

_____

Are you maintaining high standards for quality control? Customer service? Are your people?

_____

_____

_____

_____

Are you working in your best interests or those of your customers? Do you recognize the difference?

_____

_____

_____

_____

Do you understand this new growing enterprise? What's your next step? _____

_____

_____

_____

What actions or attitudes of yours, or your managers, have changed? What's the effect? _____

_____

_____

_____

Are you prudent with excess capital? Have you developed a conservative financial plan for your business?

_____

_____

_____

_____

the world outside your office. Do that and you will certainly miss issues and indicators that may affect your business, if not today, certainly tomorrow. The adept businessperson is always alert, always seeking information, and always in positive forward motion.

MONEY TO BURN

Another hazard many businesspeople don't give much thought to is the day they have excess capital. They may budget for it, but they don't prepare for it. Then the day comes; they've got more money coming in than going out.

I hear you saying, "Now that particular hazard I can handle. No problem." Perhaps you can, but the question that needs answering is how. What are your current thoughts on it? What exactly will you do when your business begins to generate more cash than it needs? Make a few notes now to yourself.

_____

_____

_____

_____

There are two distinct schools of thought on managing cash. One says, "Don't put all your eggs in one basket." The other advises, "Put all your eggs in the one basket — AND WATCH THE BASKET." Sound cash management falls somewhere between.

Let's look at some common mistakes made by small businesses with money to burn.

(a) *They strip the business:* Some entrepreneurs can't wait to take the money out of the business. Often they do this far too soon and without any concern for the company's long-term requirements. And it costs! Every time money moves, the tax collector bites. Be sure you don't give that collector one cent more than is due.

(b) *They overspend within the business:* There's a million ways to waste cash within the company, and when there's extra in the bank, some businesspeople find every one of them. Overnight they turn from cost-conscious, price-comparative buyers into certifiable buyaholics. They redo offices, lease luxury cars, organize seminars in Bali, and delude themselves that it's all for the good of the business. Sure.

(c) *They make unwise, unprofitable investments:* An ill-conceived acquisitions program is probably the best example of an unwise investment. They start throwing around words like lateral expansion plans and buying into synchronous product lines. The business owner inspired to spend money this way should prepare for a flash fire. A poorly thought-out acquisition burns cash so fast you won't see smoke.

In the course of operating a successful business, you will face decisions on what to do with your profits. You may decide to take money out for personal reasons, reinvest in your own company, upgrade your facilities and equipment, or invest outside the company. There is nothing intrinsically wrong with any of those decisions. Each may be wise depending on the company's current financial position. The key is moderation, not an exciting concept, but one that will serve your bank balance well in the long term. It simply means avoiding extremes. Cash is patient. It can sit comfortably in the bank until the process of rational decision making is complete.

When you choose to borrow money from a bank, the bank's people will work within institutionally developed guidelines that will provide them with the key business ratios in your industry sector. These include ratios on cost of goods sold, receivable turnover, working capital, profit margins, debt to equity, and more. What they are looking for is a picture of where you stand in relation to your industry as a whole. From this background data — as well as current accurate information supplied by you — the bank will decide how much and under what conditions they will loan you money. Their aim is objectivity.

If you are interested in this kind of information on your business, check with Dun and Bradstreet. If you provide them with a financial statement, they will do an individual comparison on all key ratios to companies of a similar size and asset base and provide you with a report.

Unfortunately, there are no such helpful guidelines to tell you when to take money out of your company or how much to leave in. As always, it is your decision. But here are some rules to help you make sound judgments.

(a) Take the time to think, plan, and forecast. Don't feel compelled to spend or invest before you have done your homework.

(b) Don't take profits for granted. Nothing in this world is guaranteed — least of all profits! To think otherwise is dangerous false confidence.

(c) Study and understand your financial statements. Check that balance sheet. Be certain of your company's current financial state before you set about to change it.

(d) Budget well into the future for your cash needs. The future is expensive. Look to it and don't underestimate!

(e) Never make impulsive investment decisions. Recognize your emotional pull to an investment and balance it with cool logic. Your chance to prosper lies between.

(f) Seek professional advice. Consult with your accountant and respected colleagues. There are tax regulations affecting virtually every financial decision you make, and only dedicated professionals are abreast of them. A good money manager always has one eye on the tax collector — hopefully in the rearview mirror.

So take good care of that hard-earned cash in the best way you know how. Remember too that you didn't earn those profits all by yourself; you had a lot of help. You won't go wrong by developing a plan to share the company's rewards with the people who helped create them.

BRANCHING OUT

When the small business gets too big for its hometown britches, the adventurous owner looks for new worlds to conquer. He or she scans the horizon and plans the company's first branch operation. So begins a whole new challenge, management by phone, fax, memo, and modem.

It's a heady feeling charting new territories and striding into a brighter, expanded future. If, after careful market analysis, you've decided your business will work just as well in Albany as it does in Vancouver, there's not a reason in the world not to use this method of growth for your enterprise. As with any new move, put your thinking cap on, sit in a quiet place, and do the mental work necessary to, as much as possible, anticipate new situations. Management by remote control requires organization, a new emphasis on communications, and a heightened awareness of people.

It's not enough to open the branch, set up a manager, tell him or her to hire some staff, and get back to you when the profits start rolling in. Most small business entrepreneurs I know who have established branches in other cities were taxed to the limit while building them into profitable, worthwhile operations. In almost all cases, it took them longer and cost them more than they originally projected. Unaware of the new subtleties in managing people and events from a distance, they not only underestimated travel and communication costs, they misjudged how long it would take for the branch to shape itself into a cohesive, productive unit. The learning curve was costly.

If you are considering this horizontal expansion for your enterprise, be realistic. Focus hard on your intended market, and study it from all angles.

(a) Do your market research. Is there room for your business there? Who are your competitors? Has anyone else tried and failed? Why?

(b) Plan your cash flow carefully. How much will it cost for the first year? For the second? Are your pockets deep enough?

I urge anyone considering opening a remote location to make their forecast as conservative as a Swiss banker's suit. If you must err, err on the side of caution. Any new venture, and a branch operation is certainly that, can be a dizzying cash drain if things do not go well.

LONG-DISTANCE RELATIONSHIPS

Given distance, and often time changes as well, it is difficult to establish the close working relationships and timely communication that exist automatically almost from the beginning in the founding office. Often people working in the branch feel removed from the action — cut off from the decisions and plans so readily communicated to the people in the founding office. Such feelings foster discontent and create a breeding ground for negativity. Emerson described discontent as an "infirmity of will." Not exactly what you need to ensure a robust, profitable branch.

By not planning for branch management needs, by brashly assuming the remote office will run as smoothly and on the same fuel as head office, you're setting yourself up for problems and disappointment — expensive disappointment.

For your expansion to be successful, you must —

(a) describe branch objectives and activities clearly so that both branch and head office staff have a thorough understanding of each other's aims and responsibilities.

(b) create qualified, capable management. Prepare to invest in the management people you need to attain your goals. Work from day one to forge a team of people that will ensure the branch's future.

(c) establish clear reporting lines. Wherever possible give branch people more than one person they can call on for particular problems. Try never to make them wait for answers.

(d) ensure information flows easily and directly to the branch. With today's communication technology, there is no excuse for poor or late-breaking news to remote sites. They're as near as the closest fax or keyboard.

(e) accept differences. It won't be long before your branch manager tells you, "It's different here in Albany." He or she is telling you that what works in your location needs alteration to work at theirs. Believe them. Adjust your thinking if possible. It may not make sense to you, but they're probably right.

(f) monitor quality of support provided to the branch. Remote management needs more support than local management, particularly in the start-up phase. Whether that support is in product training, administration, or marketing, ensure they get the tools and information they need to do the job you've given them.

If you plan to expand your business to another city, be clear-eyed and organized and acknowledge the difficulties in running an operation that you cannot see or touch on a daily basis.

Chapter Review

Keep your guard up and your vision keen as your organization grows. Not only are there potholes on the way to the top, there are risks when you get there. The proactive decision-maker stays alert to the changes success brings to the organization. He or she knows that every action, good or bad, has a reaction and that reaction is dealt with more easily and constructively if it is considered in advance.

- There is no substitute for honesty and equity in the workplace.

- Stay alert to the influences that affect your business; success does not mean you are invincible.

- Manage excess cash as if there is a tomorrow.

8
LEADERSHIP

. . . the good leader must have ethos, pathos and logos. The ethos is his moral character, the source of his ability to persuade. The pathos is his ability to touch feelings, to move people emotionally. The logos is his ability to give solid reasons for an action, to move people intellectually.

Mortimer Adler

As an entrepreneur, you choose to define success in your own terms, to forge a path of your own making. At the start you travel alone, you travel light, and you travel fast. It is an exciting, often perilous road, but your energy and enthusiasm carry you easily to that first plateau. You find success.

But look around. You're no longer alone. While you may have started out simply marching to a different drummer, now you're the leader of a band. You are surrounded by people, people looking to you for guidance and direction in their working lives. You are now a leader, and it's a role you may not have given much thought to when you were packing for the trip.

QUALITIES OF A LEADER

What is leadership? Can it be categorized, taught, and then easily assimilated? The answer is a definite maybe in a sea of ifs.

You can learn to be an effective leader if you have the following characteristics:

(a) *You despise injustice.* Leaders are fair. They don't reward themselves at the expense of their people. They don't dole out perks to favorites. They don't take advantage of employees. They pay fairly and they reward generously in both hard cash and recognition.

(b) *You welcome responsibility.* Leaders understand their role and freely accept its obligations. They do their job. They don't shirk obligations or pass them off while they hit the links or enjoy a three-hour lunch. They never blame others for their defeats or failures.

(c) *You have a vision.* Leaders are propelled by the future. They are not bound by present circumstances or fettered by detail. They don't survive on old glory and yesterday's bottom line. They are action oriented and on the forward move.

(d) *You can share that vision.* Leaders are communicators. They speak plainly and honestly — always. They engage their people intellectually and emotionally. They don't ask people to follow them through a maze of ill-defined goals and foggy objectives. They don't have a secret agenda.

(e) *You believe in yourself.* Leaders are confident. They are not "look how great I am" egotists. They have an innate power that comes with building success upon success. They have pride but are not prideful.

(f) *You respect others.* Leaders honor peers and subordinates equally. They are sensitive to people's insecurities, fears, and dreams. They see whole people, not stereotypes. Mary in payroll is Mary Jones, woman, wife, and mother — not Mary, the payroll clerk.

(g) *You can give more than you expect to get.* Leaders are generous. They don't hold back on their time, their praise, or their empathy if that's what the situation calls for. And they don't sit in a big chair, in a big office, with a big window doing a small job. Leaders work.

(h) *You are committed to the future.* Leaders pledge themselves to the future. They keep it firmly in sight and don't allow themselves to get tamped into the present by anxiety, fear, or uncertainty. They are active.

(i) *You have a cool head.* Leaders have composure. They don't crack, flail about, or hide in their office when things go wrong. They know it is at those times that leadership is needed most.

(j) *You can be trusted.* Leaders are straight shooters — always and in all things.

When all the verbiage is tilled under, your leadership will be judged by the strength and effectiveness of your followers. Strong, able people follow strong, able leaders. As Max Depree says in his wonderful book, *Leadership Is An Art,* "The measure of leadership is not the quality of the head, but the tone of the body." The effective leader's first concern must always be the health and well-being of that body.

Leadership is a privilege granted by those who choose to follow. The truth is, you can't lead a horse to water if it doesn't want to go (it is, after all, a whole lot bigger than you), and you can't make good people follow you if you're small-minded, miserly, and tyrannical. The best you can do is boss them around until they locate a convenient exit. Until they do, they expend minimal effort on your behalf. You lose and the company loses. That's not leadership, it's corporate vandalism.

The power to hire and fire, to promote or demote, or to raise or lower wages gives you workplace power; it does not make you a leader. Only heart and desire can do that.

Your business is a work in progress — as are you. To become what you must become to do your job fully and well, you cannot remain the same. You must nurture and enhance all your talents — none of which is more important than leadership.

119

ONE LAST THOUGHT

If you're a bull rider, you measure success in seconds — sit for just eight of them on top of that thrashing mountain of a beast and you've done your job.

Eight seconds.

It doesn't seem like much, but the bull rider needs courage to get on that bull, stamina to stay in control, and skill to go the distance. It's a bumpy ride.

Starting a business takes courage, and running it when the going gets tough certainly requires stamina, but going the distance and managing its growth demands skill and plenty of it.

That skill can be learned. Making changes in how we think, how we react, how we do things is mentally and emotionally strenuous but not impossible.

It's done one second at a time.

I wish you every success.

APPENDIX
RATIO CALCULATIONS

1. Current ratio $= \dfrac{\text{Current assets}}{\text{Current liabilities}}$

2. Quick ratio $= \dfrac{\text{Current monetary assets}}{\text{Current liabilities}}$

3. Accounts receivable turnover $= \dfrac{\text{Sales}}{\text{Average accounts receivable}}$

4. Number of day's sales $= \dfrac{365}{\text{Accounts receivable turnover}}$

5. Inventory turnover $= \dfrac{365}{\text{Average inventory}}$

6. Number of days' inventory $= \dfrac{365}{\text{Inventory turnover}}$

7. Accounts payable turnover $= \dfrac{\text{Purchases}}{\text{Average accounts payable}}$

8. Average payment period $= \dfrac{365}{\text{Accounts payable turnover}}$

9. Operating cycle $= \dfrac{\text{Number of days sales +}}{\text{Number of days inventory}}$

10. Debt ratio $= \dfrac{\text{Total liabilities}}{\text{Total assets}}$

11. Debt equity ratio $= \dfrac{\text{Total liabilities}}{\text{Owner's equity}}$

12. Profit margin $= \dfrac{\text{Net income}}{\text{Sales}}$

13. Return of assets $= \dfrac{\text{Net income}}{\text{Average total assets}}$

14. Return on investment $= \dfrac{\text{Net income}}{\text{Owner's equity beginning of year}}$

121

BIBLIOGRAPHY

Andrews, Kenneth R. *The Concept of Corporate Strategy.* Homewood, Illinois: Irwin Inc., 1987.

Batten, J.D. *Tough Minded Management.* New York: American Management Association, 1963.

DePree, Max. *Leadership is an Art.* New York: Dell Publishing, 1989.

Drucker, Peter F. *Managing for Results.* New York: Harper and Row, 1964.

Fritz, Roger. *Think Like a Manager.* Shawnee Mission, Kansas: National Seminars Publications, 1991.

McCormack, Mark H. *What They Don't Teach You in Harvard Business School.* New York: Bantam, 1984.

ANOTHER TITLE IN THE SELF-COUNSEL BUSINESS SERIES

PRACTICAL TIME MANAGEMENT
How to get more things done in less time
by Bradley C. McRae

Here is sound advice for anyone who needs to develop practical time management skills. It is designed to help any busy person, from any walk of life, use his or her time more effectively. Not only does it explain how to easily get more things done, it shows you how your self-esteem will improve in doing so. More important, emphasis is placed on maintenance so that you remain in control. Whether you want to find extra time to spend with your family or read the latest bestseller, this book will give you the guidance you need — without taking up a lot of your time! $7.95

Some of the skills you will learn are:

- Learning to monitor where your time goes
- Setting realistic and attainable goals
- Overcoming inertia
- Rewarding yourself
- Planning time with others
- Managing leisure time
- Planning time for hobbies and vacations
- Maintaining the new you

ORDER FORM

All prices are subject to change without notice. Books are available in book, department, and stationery stores. If you cannot buy the book through a store, please use this order form. (Please print)

Name _____

Address _____

_____

Charge to: ❑Visa   ❑ MasterCard

Account Number _____

Validation Date _____

Expiry Date_____

Signature_____

❑Check here for a free catalogue.

IN CANADA
Please send your order to the nearest location:
Self-Counsel Press
1481 Charlotte Road
North Vancouver, B. C.
V7J 1H1
Self-Counsel Press
8-2283 Argentia Road
Mississauga, Ontario
L5N 5Z2
IN THE U.S.A.
Please send your order to:
Self-Counsel Press Inc.
1704 N. State Street
Bellingham, WA 98225

YES, please send me:

_____copies of **Practical Time Management,** $7.95

Please add $2.50 for postage & handling.
Canadian residents, please add 7% GST to your order.
WA residents, please add 7.8% sales tax.